Praise for

ON *JOB*

"In *On Job*, Gene Fendt patiently, gently, and creatively invites readers to engage the text of the Book of *Job* by use of the venerable monastic practice of meditative reading of scripture known as *lectio divina*. Fendt helpfully exemplifies this method throughout his own exposition of one of the books of Hebrew scripture that has long posed an array of historical, linguistic, literary, and interpretive challenges to preachers, scholars, and lay readers alike. He takes due note of many of these challenges, ancient and modern, but addressing these does not distract him from what I take to be a central focus of his work: To encourage readers, by the example he provides in this work, to consider undertaking, in at least some measure, the practice of *lectio divina* as an apt instrument for breaking open the words of scripture."
—PHILIP J. ROSSI, S.J., Professor of Theology *emeritus*, Marquette University

"The Book of *Job* makes for notoriously difficult reading, for many reasons: the confusing state of the text, the seeming circularity of content and argument, the tendency of interpreters to grind assorted axes as they project their worldviews onto its characters. Gene Fendt takes a more daring, because more traditional, route: assuming the text to be inspired and coherent, with a message of utmost importance, he sits at the feet of *Job* and patiently traces its lessons on the justice of

God and of man, innocence, happiness, guilt, suffering, the wildness of sin, the paradoxes of wealth and poverty, the hard road to discovering the one thing needful. His commentary sparkles with insights that bring *Job* alive as a work of philosophical wisdom and spiritual challenge for all seekers and believers."
—PETER KWASNIEWSKI, author of *Bound by Truth: Authority, Obedience, Tradition, and the Common Good*

"G. K. Chesterton described the Book of *Job* as both a philosophical riddle and a poem. More than merely a poem, Chesterton exalted it as 'a sort of psalm or rhapsody of the sense of wonder.' Since this is so, it takes not merely a true philosopher to unlock its mystery, but a true poet. Chesterton was a true philosopher-poet; so was Thomas Aquinas; and so is Gene Fendt. This is why Dr Fendt is such an incisive guide to the bright secret of God that Job reveals 'like light seen for an instant through the crack of a closed door.' He allows us to see the secret brightness behind the mystery of suffering. He helps us to solve the riddle that the Book of *Job* sets and to see the poetry of the riddle itself. He allows us to peer through the crack of the closed door, and even prises the door open a little, revealing the light within."—JOSEPH PEARCE, author of *The Good, the Bad, and the Beautiful*

ON *JOB*
Reflections of an Accomplished Sinner
on the Suffering of the Just

⊕

But Job! At the moment when the Lord took everything, he did not say first, "The Lord took," but he said first, "The Lord gave." The word is short, but in its brevity it perfectly expresses what it wishes to indicate, that Job's soul is not crushed down in silent submission to sorrow, but that his heart first expanded in gratitude; that the loss of everything first made him thankful to the Lord that He had given him all the blessings He now took from him.

Kierkegaard

Sadness can be taken away by speaking the truth together.

St Thomas Aquinas,
Literal Exposition of Job

> ... the communication
> Of the dead is tongued with fire beyond the language
> of the living.

T.S. Eliot,
The Four Quartets

GENE FENDT

On *Job*

*Reflections of an
Accomplished Sinner on
the Suffering of the Just*

⊕

Angelico Press

First published in the USA
by Angelico Press 2024
© Gene Fendt 2024

For information, address:
Angelico Press
169 Monitor St.
Brooklyn, NY 11222
info@angelicopress.com

ISBN 978-1-62138-965-1 (pbk)
ISBN 978-1-62138-966-8 (cloth)

Cover Design: Michael Schrauzer

for my father
and
my mother

CONTENTS

Reflections
on the Book of Job

Preface from twenty-four years' distance

THERE ARE MANY WAYS of reading the Bible, and of studying it. It can be and has been read as a work of art, as history, as a source for anthropological or philosophical or theological reflection, and as the revelation of God and a mimetic impetus to prayer. And all of these ways of reading are themselves many, and therefore they interpenetrate and influence each other in innumerable ways. But it is because of the last-mentioned way of reading that the book has become, in its way, all these things to all sorts of people. For in praying and seeking God all the other ends of a person are united. In fact, even by calling it "Bible," rather than *Tanakh*, which is the Hebrew name for what Bible-readers call the Old Testament—which very name in turn gives away an orientation to something New, of which the original readers could have had at best only vague intimations—even by calling it "Bible," we announce a definite turn and direction to our reading, or a definite light into which we sight this divine kaleidoscope of books.

The grammatical complexity of that last sentence mimics, in a very small way, the complexity of reading the Bible. Since we are human, since we are affected by art, since we place ourselves in a history and know something about the history in which we stand, since we are by nature, as the

1

Greeks said, philosophers as well as the most mimetic of animals, no matter how simply we may wish to read the Bible as the revelation of God, all these others are present with and in us and it. So when any person reads the Bible, each is bringing to its pages his or her own artistic sensibilities, anthropological development, personal and cultural history, moral, philosophical, and theological virtues—in whatever state of grace or lack thereof he or she may be. This is true, in a way, of any book; but if we are reading the Bible as the revelation of God, then we are spiritually naked—and our whole being is at stake. And if it is the revelation of God, then God is present in it and we are spiritually naked before God in our reading—whether we believe it or not. Our incapacities, insensitivities, ignorance, and parochialism, as well as our sins—of omission and commission—and our hopes and lack thereof, and our weakness or lack of faith, all *exhibit themselves* in our reading. It is a frightful thing to fall into the hands of the living God: before Him who can stand?

If we were saints, this nakedness before God, and in God, would be our most perfect joy. We would find ourselves praying with St. Augustine:

> Wondrous is the depth of your words, for see, their surface lies before us, giving delight to your little ones. But wondrous is their depth, O my God, wondrous is their depth! It is awesome to look into that depth: an awe owed to honor and a trembling arising from love! (*Confessions* 12.14.17)[1]

---

[1] I will use the translation of *Confessions* by John K. Ryan; henceforth *Conf.* according to the usual scholarly format (book.chapter.paragraph).

As we grow away from being the little ones who drink milk and who reason as a child and into spiritual adulthood, it is given to us to swim in these depths, and in fact only such swimming brings us into spiritual adulthood. All the saints were formed not merely by looking at the surface of these words but by moving open-eyed in their depths. And they did so daily. And we, if we did so, would, like them, find them ever more awesome—a word which, for Augustine, is half terror, half joy, and half mystery.

If this were only a literary reading of *Job*, or some sort of historical investigation, or an artistic study of its characters and plot, or a philosophical or theological analysis, it would only be possible to exhibit a limited range of insensitivity, ignorance, or weakness; better philosophers or theologians, more knowledgeable historians, more practiced literary critics could point them out and correct them. But the aim in writing this book is what St Anselm would recognize as meditation—a meditation on, and in, the revelation of God. So, everything one is is at stake. Of his *Monologion* Anselm said that he wished to provide "a sort of pattern for meditating";[2] his meditation was groundbreaking because of its mode—it was *not* on Scripture or in it, but one of which "absolutely nothing in it would be established by the authority of Scripture."[3] Things are quite different now. Most of the modern world—especially the academic world—operates in this mode of disallowing anything to be established through the authority of Scripture by what has become unconscious habit, but there is also very little prac-

---

[2] Anselm, *Monologion and Proslogion, with the Replies of Gaunilo and Anselm*, translated by Thomas Williams (Indianapolis: Hackett, 1995), 3.
[3] Ibid.

tice of the kind of daily meditation Anselm's age usually practiced. It was that kind of scriptural meditation which shaped Anselm into one who could be asked for such a rationalist pattern without danger of him forgetting his own, more complete, shape.

We are shaped, as moderns, and even more so if we are academically trained, by such rationalist meditations and discussions, by empirical or historical investigation, without much awareness and less (if any) practice of the earlier form—*lectio divina*, out of which Anselm stepped for some moment in writing his own rational meditation. In fact, most of his day, even on those days during which he was working out his rational investigation, would have been spent in meditation on that Scripture upon which he was not explicitly depending in writing *Monologion*. This book's meditation means to provide a pattern in that earlier mode—a *lectio divina* by someone pulled by all sorts of other modern practices of which Anselm could have had no inkling. It is a way of meditating within myself and insofar as my particular shaping allows, on the revelation God grants of himself in the book of *Job*. It is written for similar modern people, formed in wholly different intellectual, aesthetic, and passional habits, to aid in slowing down, and if possible, going backwards—into that Being from whom we came to be.

This little preface is written, and then revised, a considerable time after the original project was completed; that I am able to write this preface now is partly a result of what this record of swimming in real life was. I, the writer of this late preface, am the product of this earlier writing. I thought, when I was writing it, that I was producing something, and I meant it to be, among other things, a way to honor my father and mother, a way to be with them in spirit, though distant in space. And perhaps it is that too. But it is not really a product, it is rather the linguistic surface of spiritual events, so I present it as a record of one man's meditation on one book of the Bible. And as Gregory said of his writing: "please notice that the real story has produced this spiritual offspring."[4]

While reading the Bible as a revelatory book we all do as Augustine said: "All of us who read strive to trace out and understand what he whom we read actually meant, and since we believe him to speak the truth, we do not assert that he spoke anything we know or think to be false." That being so, everyone who writes about their reading of revelation must hope for the consequence which Augustine undoubtedly prayed for concerning his own writing on Genesis: "While every man tries to understand in holy Scripture what the author understood therein, what wrong is there if anyone understand what you, O light of all truthful minds, reveal to him as true, even if the author he reads did not understand this."[5] Of course, if the author is God it will not be the case that any truth found will not be intended. Augustine is speaking of the human author, and like every human author he says

> I should have wished, had I been Moses . . . that such
> power of eloquence be given to me that not even they
> who cannot yet understand how God creates things
> would reject my words as beyond their powers; while

---

[4] Gregory the Great, *Moral Reflections on the Book of Job*, Volume 2, translated by Brian Kerns, OCSO (Collegeville, MN: Liturgical Press, 2015), 32.

[5] *Conf.* 12.18.27.

they who can already understand, no matter what true interpretation they have arrived at in their thought, would not find it passed over in your servant's few words; and if some other man by the light of truth had perceived a further meaning, it should not fail to be understood from those same words.[6]

I join my prayer to his, with you, for this work.

---

[6] *Conf.* 12.26.36.

Introduction

AMONG THE SELF-HELP BOOKS, *Job* is the Biblical version of "when bad things happen to good people," and, for Job, when things are bad, they are very bad. So, when suffering comes into a person's life, this book is a not uncommon prescription. This prescription is often taken before suffering really sets in, as a sort of general inoculation. The idea is old and popular that Job can somehow help us deal with our sufferings, and more generally that *Job*'s problem is, and so his story somehow can lead us through, the "problem of evil," and that that problem is in fact the book's primary theme.[1] Perhaps the main reason for this conjunction of personal suffering, philosophical problematic, and prescription to read *Job* is that it is suffering that makes the common man philosophical. The problem of evil which suffering raises certainly turns us that way: our first ques-

---

[1] Various translations of *Job* make the problem of the justification of God's ways to man more or less sharply the problem of the book. The new Oxford translation (NEB) seems to be most interested in turning the text to the philosophical problem of evil. For example, it emends 1:22 from a perfectly adequate "In all this Job did not sin, nor ascribe blame to God" (Pope, *Anchor Bible*) to "Throughout all this Job did not sin; he did not charge God with unreason." In *Job: The Victim of His People* (Stanford: University Press, 1987), René Girard says that reading the book "forces us to choose between the moral and metaphysical analysis of the problem of evil" (30); perhaps it also requires us to choose between prayerful and philosophical, unless we can make our philosophizing into prayer as Augustine and Anselm did. At any rate, translations lean; it helps to read several.

7

tion is "why?" Indeed, in the prefatory note of his *Answer to Job* Carl Jung begins by explaining that his problem with modern Christianity is, first, its theory that evil is merely a privation of the good, which he considers not to agree with the psychological findings,[2] and, second, that it is dualistic in the sense that it personifies evil in the *eternally* damned opposite of God: Satan.

There is a certain element of truth in Jung's psychological claim: One of the psychological problems suffering might well cause us when it is ours is an incapacity to understand that this suffering is a nothing, a metaphysical lack. It hurts too much to be a nothing. Jung considers that *Job* takes suffering more seriously than metaphysics seems to allow, but his exposition of *Job*, in turn, leads him into some philosophical and theological difficulties—at least for Christians. Among them, he holds that Job's underlying religious view is "*monotheistic*, as it unites the opposites [good and evil] in one God."[3] A god who includes evil as a necessary and eternal aspect of his being does not seem worthy of worship to me, nor do I think such a god would be helpful for anyone who wishes to cease from evil and do good—or even from one who honestly prays for release from suffering, much less sin. For reasons I hope will be eternally out of my ken, Jung seems to consider his view of God comforting. Jack Miles's Pulitzer Prize-winning *God: A Biography*[4] sees a similar point in *Job*; in it, he says,

[2] Carl Jung, "Answer to Job," in *Collected Works of C. G. Jung*, Volume II, 357.

[3] Ibid., 358.

[4] Jack Miles, *God: A Biography*. Mr. Miles is billed as a "former Jesuit," which by the very renunciation of religiosity seems to add a pen-

God grows up from a being "manipulated and controlled by a fiend"[5] to a more integrated personality in whom "the devil is now a permanent part of his reality."[6] Miles is producing a Jungian developmental psychological story for our originally less than adequately unified God. Jung's problem with modern Christianity—and Miles's happy developmental solution for God—is, of course, an old one; the Gnostics had the same problem (and solution). But the early Christians, to say nothing of the Jews, disagreed; the Church condemned the Gnostic use of the Gospel as heresy. Still, Gnosticism has a permanent popularity despite over two millennia of Christian criticism; it is, perhaps, a permanent rationalizing temptation, and it is right for Jesuits (such as Miles) who embrace it to leave their order.

These little comments about Jung, Jack Miles, and *Job* should be read as a sort of parable. When we, or those closest to us, are suffering and it becomes personally important for us to consider the meaning or lack of meaning in this suffering, we do not have to go very far in our thought or questioning about what is happening to be in very deep philosophical or theological and even psychological water— or to find that we ourselves are being plumbed. You might not think that such an immediate and pending problem would so quickly put you into heresy, or on a deep and widening rift between religious traditions or among psychological theories. That all seems so intellectual, so abstract, so far removed from the slow filling up of the lungs, the metasta-

---

umbra of authority. But what is a penumbra save a loss of light, the shadow of a shadow?

[5] Jung, "Job," 309.
[6] Ibid., 327.

9

sizing of rogue cells, the invisible sources of pain. But perhaps God and the devil have really been that close all along,
never merely intellectually interesting considerations for
those few well-educated and rather strange thinkers who
have time for them—rather, the game has been afoot for
some time, we have been floating on their currents for all of
our lives, and now it is time to pay attention—if ever we
will.

But I did not begin to (re-)read Jung's reflections on *Job*
until I was well into the work of this book. I mention him
here as one example of the kind of reading *Job* generally
gets from the intellectual cast of reader, and even where
reading might lead an ordinary thinking person. There is,
of course, a great gap between the intellectual life and the
spiritual life, though some people (mostly intellectuals)
often mistake the one for the other. The Book of Job itself
might itself stand as an emblem of that wide disjunction;
for of all the books which have come into the world
through that most intellectual, and arguably most spiritual,
of all peoples, the Jews, the Book of Job seems to have been
least carefully preserved, copied, and edited—or perhaps it
is only the most fought-over and divisive. There are more
than the usual number of places where the received text
seems senseless, broken, improperly ordered, or just missing to scholars of the Biblical languages.[7] This was something I discovered early in my parallel reading of trans-

---

[7] I here speak not only of the named Biblical scholars whose work
on *Job* I have examined: Hugh Anderson in *The Interpreter's One-Volume
Commentary on the Bible*, Marvin H. Pope in *The Anchor Bible: Job*, Robert A. Watson in *The Expositor's Bible*, R.A.F. MacKenzie, SJ, in *The Jerome Biblical*, Samuel Terrien and Paul Scherer in *The Interpreter's Bible*;

lations and commentators—and I found it, at first, rather surprising. Of the inspired Hebrew books, the one on the most openly philosophical problem is arguably the most shattered. This is so much the case that, at certain points in the text, use of two or three different translations will reveal no agreement even about who is speaking the line, or where the lines belong. You would think that intellectuals would take better care; you would think that copiers of a sacred text would not dare to edit and redact so strongly. The debates about *Job*'s age relative to the rest of the Jewish canon allow a gamut of reasonable opinion, and that unsettled debate is merely a superficial historical problem: it seems that the small piece of ground which is this text has inspired as many wars as the holy city itself—and as internecine: destructive even of the text. I began to wonder if perhaps the war between the intellectual and the spiritual tendencies of the Hebraic soul, and so of man's, might not here have left its most considerable traces. But if a book is inspired by God, I suppose that means *God* is attempting to get us somewhere through it, not that *we* are to take it somewhere, or are to use it to get somewhere with someone else, or that we are, through it, to solve a problem of our own devising.

Self-help, philosophical and theological problem, interest in the text and story, but first of all, meditation and prayer:

but also those unnamed fieldhands and foot soldiers whose work is visible in the footnotes of every translation. I have examined the following translations: RSV (1952), Today's English Version (1976), Confraternity-Douay (1963), Anchor (1973), Authorized (King James) (1611), the New English Bible (1970), and the New Jerusalem Bible (1985). My quotations vary among the standard contemporary translations, except where pointed out explicitly.

On *Job*

I entered upon this project with all this mixture of motives. I myself wonder whether such impurity of heart is not (yet another) sign against me, and whether my reflections will be of value to any other human being beside myself. I hope that such a mixture of motives as my own is not necessarily a bad thing, for our prayers are human, and so our nakedness reveals blackheads, scars, and numerous wild hairs, and our meditations attempt to allow our complete humanity to be lit up by God. To the extent that I have done that, these reflections might then also be valuable to someone else. So.

My father, the day after the first of several strokes, was diagnosed with terminal stage-four adenocarcinoma. It was in both his lungs and his spine, and the strokes were apparently secondary to the cancer, which had changed his blood chemistry. Since my university duties kept me farther away from home than the rest of my family, I assigned myself the task of reading a part—generally one chapter—of *Job* each Friday, in a manner that would approximate the medieval tradition known as *lectio divina*. It was my hope to in some way be united to my father's suffering; it is my hope that this book might help other readers practice that age-old tradition. According to that tradition—one of the regular forms of monastic prayer—the reading of the sacred text, usually aloud and several times (the *lectio*), would be followed by *meditatio*—a consideration of some of its important words, images, occurrences. My method was to read several of the different English translations, which would imprint the section for the day strongly on my mind, then turn to several of the more exacting scholars, to learn what I could of how the original language was working. In this way each Friday I considered one portion of the book and, so far as I could, sat on the words and phrases, turning them over with the scholars who knew them better. For over a millennium a significant portion of the world was set to regular rhythms of *ora et labora* (prayer and work), so, on Fridays, when I did not have to teach, I aimed at a similar sort of *lectio* and *meditatio.* This beginning led the monk to *oratio* and *contemplatio*—from reading and meditation to prayerful response and contemplation of the word. The purpose of this method of prayer, as with all others, is to come consciously into the presence of God, in whom we live and move and have our being, and from whom comes every good thing. It was the only thing I could think of to do, and it was through this prayer that I hoped to unite myself with my father and mother during their suffering.

As already noted, I have a professional interest in the problem of evil, and I confess to remembering the book only in its large and vague Masterplot outline—that shape to which unmeditative reading sooner rather than later reduces. I knew the book presented many philosophical, theological, and psychological (as well as literary) problems—the kind of thing I always find interesting, perhaps as a very elite form of escapism, as not a few people like to suggest of scholarly pursuits in general. But I entered upon this reading wishing to be taught; I hoped the time would be—well, would let God teach what He would, and so redeem the time.

I (finally) also must confess to not being perfectly faithful; I looked for excuses some Fridays; the modern world offers many, and soon enough I found them. The book of Job is difficult, hard to read for a number of probably conflicting reasons; in places I was bored, found Job and his friends a drag to be around, and thought the book redundant and in need of an editor who could cut to the chase. The book, then, is a lot like suffering itself; a lot like dying. Given the choice I would rather be excused: suffering, too, is difficult, hard to read, boring, and redundant. Sometimes you just want to get it over with; but it isn't done with you yet. But more often than not, opening *Job* and beginning to read and think about what he or his interlocutors were saying led into thoughts and feelings I had not expected. And then, frequently, the thought and spirit of Job demanded my time on Saturday or Sunday or Thursday—as importunate as suffering. It was humbling and glorious; I could not have spent the time any better. I have done much worse.

From early on I saw that if *Job* was dealing with the problem of evil and was somehow to be a consolation in times of trouble, it was not going to offer an easy answer or consolation for me, and I began to wonder if, in fact, that was its purpose at all. Perhaps, in a time of suffering, thinking about the suffering works it deeper—and this is to be desired. But who could desire this? Expecting a consolation or expecting a philosophical problem to be posed and answered, I discovered instead that I was undergoing an examination. It is very hard to read this book meditatively; much more difficult than reading it for scholarly purposes. The difficulty is not that it "goes over our heads because . . . [it points to] the archetypes of the collective unconscious" (Jung, 362). The difficulty is, rather, a difficulty of conscience. I felt as if I were being probed by a very long finger, and weighed, and found wanting. It does not go over our heads; it goes into the corners of our souls, and the basement, and the secret rooms. This is the record of that reading. I think the most useful way to use this book is to read a chapter of *Job*, and then, as an aid to meditation, read a chapter of this "pattern" for a modern *lectio divina*— which, as in other times, aims to lead further in—into the revelation itself. What comes of such reading will not be up to me, or to you. To read either *Job* or this book just to be done with either will probably not do much. I offer this, then, as a pattern for meditation.

JOB I

Something Like a Fairy Tale

THE BOOK OF JOB has a beginning that is something like a fairy tale; it might easily—with little change of narrative tone—be told to children: "Once upon a time in the land of Us there lived a man named Job who was faithful to God, a good man who never did evil." Job's name, according to Elie Wiesel, "means: where is father—where is our father."[1] I am unsure whether he is speaking parabolically about the book, or has found a poetic echo to Job's name in Hebrew which the more traditional Biblical scholars do not note. It is a good parable to put into Job's name, for the first question we might ask in the suddenness of suffering is where our father is. Or some time into the suffering, "why have you abandoned me?" The father's name might itself be a question, then, for Job is himself a father, and the question is not about him. We know where this father is. He has seven sons and three daughters—a large-sized family, but not so excessive that the children could be thought of only in bunches lacking individuality, as must be the case with

---

[1] Elie Wiesel, "Job," in *Peace, in Deed: Essays in Honor of Harry James Cargas*, 119. Several of Wiesel's own books, based on his experiences as a teenager in Auschwitz and Buchenwald, echo themes in *Job*: in particular *Night* and *The Trial of God*. His father and mother and a younger sister did not survive; two other sisters did.

Something Like a Fairy Tale

some ancient and modern tribal kings, and as perhaps was
so for those long-lived generations between Adam and
Noah, where only the chosen son is named—"and then he
lived 800 years and had other children" (Gen 5:4). Job's was
a happy family, one in which the children took turns giving
feasts, to which all the sons and daughters would come.
The number of Job's happiness is ten, the number signifying perfection—for it summarizes all the law: seven, the
number of commands regarding the neighbor; three, those
signifying dedication to God. And his familial happiness is
surrounded by multiples of perfection—the animals (seven
thousand sheep, three thousand camels...) are nature's halo
around the just man.

Though biblical scholars generally deny it and the story
does not say, I like to think that Job and his wife perhaps
were with the children for the occasional feast, but the story
does tell us that every morning after a feast Job would get up
early and offer sacrifices for each of his children to purify
them, lest by some unintentional fault they might have
sinned. What is clear, and what we can say without import-
ing anything foreign into the social interactions of Job's day,
is that the round of feasts is a week, and if the sons "each on
his day" supply the feast, we can understand that Job's family accomplishes a liturgical mimesis of God's creative work.
As each day is given its work by God, so each son takes up
on his day the appropriate feast of praise. The familial and
social world, under the patriarchy of Job, is the liturgically
perfect response to the world created by God as a gift. If we
read each son giving a feast "on his day" not as the annual
birthday but as an assigned day of each week, then Job's
family accomplishes what Plato set forth as a law for the
well-founded city, that there shall be exactly 365 festival days

17

in honor of the heavenly powers (*Laws* 828b). It is no wonder that nature is a fruitful halo in Job's world. The Hebrew
text is, apparently, ambiguous: perhaps Job offers his sacrifice of atonement each day, perhaps he offers it on the
morning of the first day, after the round of feasts has con-
cluded, before the next begins. But for what is he atoning?

What Job must have been afraid of was that his children
might not be thankful enough for all they had received,
that they might not have been thanking God for every deli-
cious mouthful and every morsel and moment of joy
together. Like Job, his children know where every good
thing comes from, but Job offers his purificatory sacrifice
because one or another might have at some moment of
their happy feast day forgotten the presence of God, and so
unintentionally insulted the giver of the feast, present yet
invisible. Job's sacrifice is made lest his children enjoy their
good gifts for themselves rather than use the gifts in celebratory enjoyment of the divine giver. Job's life is a constant
liturgy; this is its perfection, the picture of his wealth is its
visible halo, an impasto of gold to draw our attention and
instigate our wonder.

Job does not *know*, indeed he does not even suspect, that
any of his children have been at any moment less than perfectly grateful, less than perfectly faithful or responsive to
the giver of the feast; he thinks that one of them might
inadvertently have been so.[2] But if he did know that one of

---

[2] Wiesel suggests that Job had neglected the education of his children; they are having such a good time that Job is afraid of punishment.
He puts this together with the fact that Job's virtues are listed in the
order inverse from the usual, perhaps indicating that his real motive is
fear of sin ("Job," 121). But to start with perfection and go down to the

them had been for a moment ungrateful, and perhaps not inadvertently—though how anyone as blessed as his children could be so purposefully ungrateful as to neglect, much less to curse, God would be a terrible mystery to Job—if any of them had been so, had done so, what would Job not have voluntarily sacrificed to keep his child safe from the eternal memory of that ingratitude? What would he not have suffered to spare his child from the just wrath of the lord of heaven and earth? Would he not willingly suffer the loss of all his property, his health, even his life? Is that not what his early and daily sacrifices mean? For Job worshipped God and was faithful to Him. Nothing could be more important to Job than this: that his children be as constantly grateful to God as he.

But of what am I speaking? There is not even the breath of this scandal. In his fear of even a moment's forgetfulness Job's holiness appears. He is absolutely concerned about even the smallest thing in this regard. To be ungrateful or forgetful of one's parents or the good one has received from

smallest virtue might in fact imply that Job is careful all the way down to the least thing; his greatness did not go to his head, so that he exhibits the best and highest qualities but has feet that go all the way to earth about the lesser ones. So, then, the happiness of his children's feasts exhibits the blessing on Job, not the questionability of his virtue, which God, in any case, considers unmatched. Wiesel also mentions the Talmudic and Midrashic sources which say that Job was an advisor of Pharaoh's who, when asked whether the Jews should be freed, said nothing. "Neutrality is always sinful for it helps the oppressor, never his victims. That is why he was punished" ("Job," 122). Perhaps Wiesel is looking for a way to find fault with Job in order to understand what comes next. A late version of Job's visitors. God says otherwise to the Satan: "there is none like him upon the earth" (1:8). And at the end, of Job's friends: "they have not spoken rightly of me, as Job has" (42:7).

other human beings in the constant flow of human interaction is both forgivable and forgettable, for our debts in regard to all of these are relative, and our memories decay with our bodies. Job's concern is over a debt that is absolute, the debt of creation, the good of being and being able to know God; to be forgetful or ungrateful is to forget that one exists and is able to know God, or to wish not to be and to wish not to be able to know God. That wish is impossible for Job to imagine, so his fear is of the momentary forgetfulness, the kind of thing that, among men, is excusable, a trifle, and has but small importance even among things relative. But in regard to God constant gratitude is but our duty. This Job knows, even if we—his children—are more constantly forgetful. There was no one like Job in his time, for his happiness lay in his constant gratitude, which is his constant awareness of God; his gratitude is so constant it is purificatory. Upon such as these the weight of creation rests.

To think about Job, even in this happy time, is to feel something of that weight. Who could accept this burden of constant gratitude? The weight of constant awareness of grace, of God's gifts? After only *writing* this much I prefer to stop for a while and take a nap so that I might forget this thought, but Job *rises up early* to offer sacrifices for each of his children, by name. To do so is his happiness. May your sacrifice be acceptable for me, too, Job; let me turn the other way on my pillow. I do not wish to seem ungrateful, but I do not wish to have gratitude as my constant and ever-present task. But what does this feeling really mean? It means I wish for part of my life to be absolutely independent, not a gift, but mine to give, to use, to spend, to sleep upon—to offer on the altar of another god: Aphrodite,

Apollo, Dionysos, or perhaps some modern name. I want my self to be my own. I wish to be independently wealthy, not to be living on capital given by someone else—someone to whom, even if he would say, "do whatever you like, there is no need for accounting," I would with every penny at least still owe the unaccounted-for debt of gratitude. Far better to say thank you once and for all, or perhaps on the anniversary of the gift send a card; but to be in debt for absolutely everything at every moment, even for the word of thanks, even for the capacity to utter it, the capacity for the lips and tongue to move as the heart and mind direct—who can bear this? But Job does not merely bear it, Job is happy. As happy as Francis of Assisi naked and begging for old corn. As happy as Thomas Aquinas, who, rising for matins, writes of his happy love until three, until six in the morning, and then goes out to teach. Already Job is too much for me. There is none like him upon the earth.

For gratitude is not at all a weight to Job, not at all a burden. *He gets up early*, and this is the first thing he does. He gets up early—as if the day after the feast, or the round of feasts, is the day of great celebration. He gets up early—as Abraham did one well-known morning (Gen 22:3)—and he sacrifices once for each of them, not by rote, but by name. And the numbers themselves restate the perfection of Job's sacrifices: seven signifying completeness, the unity of odd and even, the trinity of heaven united to the four elements of creation. Job's life is a conscious participation in and reminiscence of that creation, of the constant repetition of the seven days—the things and Sabbath rest of time proceeding from and returning to the eternal word. And ten children: the number of the law and perfection of life; the three women standing for the commands oriented to

21

contemplation and fear of the Lord, the seven men lining out the responsibilities of the social life (and fulfilling them, each on his day)—eschewing evil. And the women are always made a part of the feast, as if every element of the social life is imbued with contemplative prayer. Martha and Mary are not in separate rooms fulfilling separate duties in this family life. And this life has its source in Job, in his perfect justice; he is its father; and Job's gratitude is eager, he names his gifts individually, it is perfect and complete; Job joins heaven to earth each day, early. Gratitude is not a weight, but an exaltation.

The folk or fairy tale aspect of the Job story reverberates through the fabulous counting up of his herds: "seven thousand sheep, three thousand camels, five hundred yoke of oxen, five hundred she-asses, and a great number of work animals, so that he was greater than any of the men of the East" (1:3). There is no counting the number of servants, no estimate of the number of tents, the number of families, the number of servant-children who both share in and are part of Job's wealth. And as with all fabulous wealth there is no story of how it was accumulated. There is only a boundary condition: Job was careful not to do anything evil, so much so that he will say later that no man can make a case against him. God, we will soon discover, agrees. We must believe, then, that to the traveler Job gave refreshment, to the homeless and unemployed a home and employment, to the hungry food, to the sick comfort, to the outcast and distressed refuge and respect. If he fears even a passing instant of forgetfulness of God on the part of his children, how could he do less than all these things himself—at every turn of opportunity? And again Job is too much—at every turn of opportunity. At every turn. He must go out into the highway to look for those in need so they will not have to suffer the embarrassment, the indignity of coming to beg. Have you marked my servant Job? There is none like him upon the earth. A parallel question: have you seen Humility?—she is out looking for you.

⊕

"When the day came for the sons of God to present themselves before the Lord, the adversary also came along with them" (1:6). With this shift of venue, the earthly boundaries of Job's story, pressed to the limit by the fabulous wealth and constant gratitude, are entirely evaporated: we can no longer be sure of the separation, of where the earthly ends and the heavenly begins. Suddenly we are at a particular day in heaven during the legendary once-upon-a-time of Job—heaven's time is folded into earth's story. This is exactly the opposite of the usual consideration of the connection of heaven and earth. Even knowing the story, knowing what is to come, we are already marvelously comforted, for the human time of Job is not just a drop in the eternal ocean of God's life, but this human time has *within it* one of the celebratory days of heaven, a day when all the sons of God present themselves to the Lord. A particular Sabbath in Job's life was a day in which all the sons of God appear before the Lord. Who would wish for a royal wedding, or a millennial change in their lifetime, could one of their days be such a day as this—the day when all the sons of heaven present themselves? And just like Job's children, all the sons of God come to present themselves at the feast—even the black sheep of the heavenly family, who answers just like any wayward son or daughter when asked where he's been: "Oh, here and there, roaming the face of the earth" (1:7). The question is asked as if by a father who knows, and answered as if by a child who knows that the father knows the answer. In a comic tale the parent would ask, "Did you happen to see Paddy at the pub then?" It is almost that clear; he has been roaming to and fro in the earth; no doubt then that the adversary has been offered Job's refreshment. God knows where he's been and what he's been up to, and so he asks directly: "Have you noticed my servant Job, how there is none like him on the earth, blameless and upright. . . ?" (1:8).

Knowing this child of God, the roaming one, the one who, on the day when the sons of God appear, shows up as if by accident, as if just in the neighborhood—knowing this one intimately—I know what he doesn't want to notice and what he doesn't want to have noticed: he has appeared on the commanded day. God, quite naturally and agreeably, doesn't notice. He plays along with the wayward one's wishful thought that he can wander freely and entirely of his own accord; He pays no attention to the fact that the adversary has in fact *shown up* on the day appointed, but presumes it is the accidental visitation of someone with no particular place to go or ax to grind—the wandering of the man of independent means. God seems pleased by this surprise visitation, as if it has been awhile and the two of them have much to catch up on. But if God seems to accept at face value the accidental nature of the free spirit's visitation, His question is a subtle reminder of what the spirit wishes to forget, for to notice Job at all is to notice his constant gratitude, his glorious awareness of infinite debt, his knowledge (we might say) *of what day it is.* Job, for all his wealth, has never entertained the idea of independence from God.

Naturally the free spirit can—if need be—admit to gratitude; not to do so would be small and slavish *ressentiment*, but to be constantly grateful—what is that but an admission of dependence? And so, like anyone who does not wish to admit to a good immediately before him, he does not answer God's question directly but makes an excuse for the existence of the good—as if it were a fault. There is a kind of petulance in the satan's response that arises from recognizing that someone who is in some way equal or inferior has surpassed us, and has surpassed us precisely where we might have been expected to succeed. For to make an excuse for something's existence is to recognize that existence; and, in the moral realm, if a characteristic is not a fault, then the fault is not to have it. So the satan does not answer directly the question about the goodness of Job, for this would involve him in a sticky moral problem in which he would not come off looking well, but it is clear from his answer that he has, in fact, noticed Job; perhaps he has stopped by several times—a particularly impertinent beggar, a trying and sickly visitor—but he has been received generously and graciously each time. Perhaps he has even been sought for on the road, so that he may be saved the shame of begging. He explains away what he has seen, but this makes it clear that he has seen it, he has seen the grateful and gracious economy of Job—indeed, writing an assigned theme on the matter could not make it any clearer. Job has everything; he can afford to be generous and thankful: "Is it for nothing he honors you? . . . the earth is full of his possessions" (1:9–10). The satan has seen Job's piety, but he reduces it to its material causes—at least he hypothesizes the cause: put forth your hand and touch all that he has, and watch the causes change the man. But along the way, despite himself, the satan speaks truly—for the world is full, as is Job's gratitude.

25

On *Job*

So God allows the adversary power over all that is Job's. Will he dare try to prove himself? Or does something in him already know he is lying?[3]

It was a commonplace of medieval criticism to point out here that "Satan cannot harm just men as much as he wishes but only as much as he is permitted. One should also consider that the Lord did not order Satan to strike Job but only gave him the power, because 'the will to do harm is in any evil man on his own, but the power is only from God.'"[4] So, wrapped in the cloak of his own will, "the satan departed from the presence of the Lord" (1:12). And these two phrases are equivalent: "wrapped in one's own will," "departing from the presence of God." The satan's theory is that if we unfold Job's piety, we will find him wrapped in his own will too. God's theory—but what am I saying?—

---

[3] Miles says that "the Lord has been tempted into making a wager with the enemy of mankind. . . . [He] is susceptible to the suggestions of a [hostile] celestial being . . . manipulated and controlled by a fiend" and that the devil introduces the higher morality of serving God for nought (*God: A Biography*, 308–9), but it is pretty clear that it is God's question which sparks the satan's resentful answer. But what does he resent already? Miles continues mistaking who is doing what throughout his essay. He says, "the Lord . . . withdraws reward and inflicts punishment" (310); he claims of the wager that "the Lord does not win it, he simply drops it" (311). But the subject of the last sentence should be the satan, and the first remark introduces rewards and punishments into a love story—a satanic introjection—and then proposes the wrong grammatical subject to boot: for it is *the satan* who suggests rewards and punishments are the way to understand love, and *he* is the inflictor of evil. Love and the world of rewards and punishments are two different worlds. It is dangerous to read books like *Job*, and dangerous to write about them.

[4] Thomas Aquinas, *The Literal Exposition on Job*, 83; Thomas is quoting the *Glossa Ordinaria* on Genesis 3:1.

God's *knowledge* is opposed to that theory. The test is invented by the adversary; the wager is made by the adversary; and the test and the wager are an attempt to exhibit that love has a cause and that the cause of love is always self-love. And love itself is a matter of honors and rewards and punishments. The wager and the test presume the truth of that hypothesis: What else could love be?

To one wrapped in his own will this is the only plausible story; such a one goes forth from the presence of God by his will, so his going from place to place in the earth is symbolic of his moral state—always going forth from the face of God—wandering here and there, following his own will. Opposing Job, the world of the satan is full of God's absence, so—in reality—nothing is his possession (for, in reality, the world is God's), and there is nothing to be grateful for. The depth of his being is to be wrapped in his own will, and this secret intention he finds in himself the adversary presumes to be present in all spirits; no doubt he presumes the purpose of creation itself is the self-glorification and self-aggrandizement of God, but to believe so is clearly marked, in *Job*, as *departing*, departing from the presence of God. Of course, to successfully prove that the secret cause is self-will would be exculpatory to a certain kind of spirit—if, in fact, he were seeking exculpation. But who would seek that? Surely to do so implies that something is owed... to someone.

Aquinas puts it this way: the satan "leaves the presence of the Lord because he withdraws from the intention of the one permitting." God permits "in order to manifest his virtue"; but the satan acts "to provoke [Job] to impatience and blasphemy" (ibid., 84). Consider, in comparison with Job, how little provocation it takes for us to... and what, thereby, is manifested of us.

27

On *Job*

⊕

When sorrows come, they come not single spies but in battalions. Before any single announcement can be finished, on a day of feasting at the house of his eldest son, everything is lost to Job save the four servants who announce the news. The wheel of fortune has turned faster than human language can say. Each of the four servants—if there are four (perhaps there is only one, a son of God who came as an importunate beggar and was given a job)—can barely finish his sentence before the next comes in to pour out more trouble. "And Job began to tear his cloak and cut off his hair, he threw himself prostrate on the ground" (1:20). But Job does not complain of God's abandonment, of being forsaken or betrayed. All good things are lost to Job; he hugs the ground. The objects of his whole life's love and care are all destroyed; he throws himself upon the ground. His tears raise insignificant clouds of dust, like tiny footsteps, as they fall upon . . . the ground. As he tears his cloak in sorrow he opens his mouth and intones that most sublime magnificat: "The Lord has given and the Lord has taken away; blessed be the name of the Lord." If gratitude is the test of all human happiness, then Job has passed his test.

The events occur with demonic speed, and the servants, with equally demonic speed, enter upon each other to spill the news. It is not said whether the four servants—if they are four—notice Job's response.

> Have you noticed My servant?
> Who is there on earth like unto Job?

28

JOB 2

Another Feast Day in Heaven

IT IS A FEAST DAY IN HEAVEN, a day when all the sons of God appear before the Lord. How many of Job's days are there between these days when the sons of God appear before Him? Is there a day between these days when Job has not appeared before the Lord? And if there is no such day for Job, how much less could there be such a day for one of the heavenly beings? According to the literal Hebrew each of Job's sons gave the feast on his own day of the week, so that each day it was assigned to one of them to prepare the feast of thanksgiving. But one of the sons of heaven has been looking for a different day—roaming the earth. So he says. We know, however, that he has been very busy in one particular place. This time every reader knows as well as God that the wayward free spirit has been exceptionally busy and in one place. Has he noticed Job? In his roaming; in going through the earth?

This time, among the sons of God, Satan not only comes along, but "presents himself";[1] he not only comes among them, but comes with them as one whose attendance is expected—presenting himself. We might consider this an improvement, but he is more probably still

[1] Norman C. Habel, *The Book of Job* (Philadelphia: Westminster Press, 1985), 77.

29

wrapped in his own will; he has made a bet and he is not so cowardly as to pretend he is not expected. But again, to the direct question he refuses direct answer, not only to the question "where have you been?" but also to "have you noticed?" To answer the latter question would imply a recognition of what Job does, and, concomitantly, what the wandering spirit does not. To answer the former honestly would require that he confess to being at the scene of several recent disasters and would imply that something important hung on the bet and that he had been paying attention to the game he has instigated very closely. Answers to such questions must, at all costs, be avoided; so he offers another *explanation* for Job: "Skin for skin! All that a man has he will give for his life, but put forth your hand and touch his bone and his flesh. . . ." Let us explain away gratitude to God that we may not be discovered to be lacking; let us make ourselves clothes to cover our nakedness. The furious business of Satan—so quickly did he act that the messengers trip each other up in reporting their news—and its unaccountable failure, is covered over by "roaming here and there" and then an explanation that the passing incidents with Job were really insignificant: you can't expect good data from an inconclusive and partial test like that.

Perhaps he is not even lying. Perhaps the adversary really thinks that the death of one's children is insignificant; this would be natural, for to think such a thing significant would be an admission of lack of independence, a confession of the extent to which one's own freedom and good is bound to the freedom and good of others—even if originally through one's own choice. That freedom might *give itself* to someone is not even imaginable to the spirit wrapped in its own will. So such a being as he is would never create a world. And such a one would further consider that a freedom bound by its own choice even where it would not choose, even in suffering—which it would not choose, even to sorrow—which it would not choose...—that kind of freedom is utterly foolish and unimaginable. A freedom which does not roam here and there about the earth even when suffering reports day after day as the assignment, a freedom that stays there and suffers—what kind of freedom is that? What kind of slavish, sickly, impotent, sluggish spirit would bear this out even to the edge of doom? The kind that loves its own life of course! The kind that is happy to escape alive—though it lose all else it still has its health and the occasional opportunity for pleasure. Thus thought the wanderer.

Job, on the other hand, holds fast to his integrity, but his integrity is not identical with his own will.

And the Lord said to the adversary, "He is in your power; only spare his life."

And the Satan went forth from the face of the Lord and smote Job... (2:6–7).

He is quick to leave; quick to smite. And so the adversary is allowed under Job's skin: "from the soles of his feet to the crown of his head" (2:7). And Job in his illness is not taken to a hospital, or cared for in a comfortable bed, or given the usual medicines; he is instead cast out beyond the walls of the city; he sits on the garbage heap and scrapes his sores with a potsherd. And even Job's wife appears to suggest the devil's business: "Why don't you curse God and die?" (2:9). Now if we were to give a psychological explanation of *Job*, here is where we should begin.

It is not necessary to think, with Jung, and more recently

with Jack Miles,[2] that God has aspects of His personality that are dark to Him, things that He needs to discover with the help of the adversary. Though He uses the word "incite" (2:3), it is not necessary to think that God is incited, like a child by a petulant adversary, against His own good friend. It is perfectly plausible to think that God here is as ironic as some think the satan is. God's irony is not an attempt to hide any meaning out of fear of discovery or avoidance of love, but to show the hider of meaning that He knows perfectly well how meaning is hid. It is perfectly sensible to hear God here mocking his waywardest son by using the wayward's own favorite game, rather than discovering a dark side of Himself, when He says, "you moved me against him, and for what—nothing? And see, he stands fast." It is not God who speaks against the wayward child, but the facts of the being in the world: "see, he stands fast. What do you make of that?" The satan has been given the *carte blanche* of freedom, God is saying, and what has he accomplished? The satan has moved everything in Job's world against him, and for what? "And see, he stands fast." The satan has been given permission for every divine power save the giving and taking of Job's own being, and what has his divine waywardness proven? "See, he stands fast." Fancy that. And perhaps this ironic mockery would incite the demon to go even further. Let him go to the very rim of being if he must (and if he has not driven Job there already); we will pick this possibility up momentarily.

If we are to talk psychologically, let us stay among the human beings: with Job and his wife. And let us recall that in *Genesis*, the creation of man is not complete until the

---

[2] Miles, *Biography*, cf. 309, 408, among others.

creation of woman. That Adam must inform God of this lack is rather humorous, but it *is* Adam who informs God of his own incompletion, for when Adam sees all the creatures and, seeing them in God, knows all their names without ever having been taught, he sees immediately that there is none that is a suitable helpmeet to him (Gen 2:20). Knowing that the temporal creature requires, besides knowledge of the eternal, some temporal aid, God answers Adam's prayer—in the flesh.[3] Adam rejoices: "At last!" Mankind knows itself and begins. St Augustine explains the psychological significance of this symbolism by saying that the whole human mind has two functions.[4] One, symbolized by Adam, is attention to the eternal; the other, symbolized by Eve, is attention to the temporal. This division was echoed inversely in the children of Job, where the women symbolized the commandments oriented to God, and the brothers the seven commands oriented to physical and social life. Both are necessary for the continued naturally proper existence of the human being. In fact, the being is not complete without both. It is as if, without Eve, Adam would not know to feed himself—would not know that he has to; and without Adam, there are just animals in the garden—none of them knowing what they are, or what for, they do not even have the distinction of names. We might, without stretching of modern or antique language, call

---

[3] I find it difficult to believe that this story is the product of human wit; it seems rather to be the source of it. Were men and women related in any other way there would be no good jokes about their relations: the jokes would be merely abusive of one side or the other (or both). Contemporary life proves the point.

[4] What follows is motivated by Augustine's discussion in *De Trinitate*, Book 12.

these two aspects of the human being wisdom and science, but the science which deals with the world is to have its head covered by wisdom, as Augustine, quoting St Paul, puts it. Sin comes to be when science forgets wisdom and turns to make itself its own good, wrapping itself in its own will, presuming no higher; or, in other words, when mankind turns from contemplation of the eternal to make the temporal world it deals with (and the sensible pleasures of which such science speaks and to which it is oriented) its entire aim and complete good. Just so, at an earlier time we must presume that Job and his wife were one flesh—as all the familial relationships echoed—but here their division is exhibited. Here she is, for the first time, introduced as a separate character, with a will divided from Job's; until this time we must assume their unity. It is as if, under the weight of this suffering, a part of himself *wishes to revolt*; a part of himself—that part oriented to the goods of the world—suggests that he curse God and die. But wisdom refuses. She is a part of himself, and until this great suffering she has not had occasion to speak differently from him; but now this part wishes to curse. And this is true about suffering, and agrees with the psychological data: under terrible suffering does not some part of us wish to revolt? To curse?[5] But do we wish this with our entire soul? Or does some part of us, at least at some time, hold us back from doing so, or judge us as failing in some way when we do?

Of course, if one considers the temporal world and its

---

[5] Dr. Rieux, in Albert Camus's novel *The Plague*, is described just this way after watching the death of the child: "He felt like shouting imprecations," to the priest he says "weariness is a kind of madness. And there are times when the only feeling I have is one of mad revolt" (218).

pleasures to be the whole and complete good, then, in lacking it, it makes sense to curse God and die—for every good thing is already lost. Job's wife suggests exactly what science can know of the truth: if you have none of the goods of the world, the world is no good to you. So, curse God and die. The psychological symbolism Augustine suggests from Genesis and St Paul is applicable, too, in *Job*. Job's wife suffers despair, and so does any other *half* of a human—male or female—which forgets that the being *who makes good* is entirely different from the beings that are made so. In the absence of all the good things of the world, can we say that all of being is bad, can we curse God? It is a logical possibility; clearly, it is an emotional possibility, certainly one wrapped in his own will *must* suggest such a thing, but if we can *ask if it is right*, if there is this slightest hesitation of the mind, must it not be because there is some other good thing operating in us—the mind's ability to judge of good and evil, which is still (is it not?) a good thing? That power, the power which knows eternal things, symbolized by the uncovered head of the man in Augustine's consideration of *Genesis* and Paul, is able to know a good not of the world, which may yet be praised in the world. And whence is *that* good thing, whence its principle and power of... hesitation even under this severe and sudden torment?

Gregory the Great enlarges this Augustinian psychology. Job is symbolic of the body of Christ, the Church, struck "with grievous persecution, not only in its last and most remote but even the highest members."[6] He continues, along lines implied by Augustine: "when Job's wife tries to get him to curse God, she indicates carnal people inside the

---

[6] Gregory the Great, *Moral Reflections*, Vol. 2, 31.

35

Church, who are the shrewd tempter's allies."[7] Just as his friends, who will be arriving shortly, such people cause anguish to the good man. Part of this anguish we must understand in Augustine's way: the man himself is anguished, for he is not a pure disembodied spirit, but an embodied soul, one whose real being is the one flesh of Job and his wife. But when we think of them as separate beings, as in Gregory's analogy to members of the Church, then the anguish must also be Job's for his wife—one member of the Church for another, who though a member has not yet fully put off the old man—and here the old man is complaining. The old man whose will is not yet fully united with Christ, of whom Job is the figure and prophecy, as Gregory says he is of the Church on earth.

Without tracing any of these thoughts so far, Job, even when prompted with the appropriate line, does not waver: "We accept good things from God; and should we not accept evil?" If the tempter's experiment proves anything, it has now proven that Job loves God for nothing, for no cause (cf. 1:9, 2:3). Job's goods and body are wholly delivered over to the adversary and the adversary fails, and we now might expect that even as he fails another feast is toward in heaven, at which the satan will appear, as usual, having his last excuse: hope lasts as long as life. So the satan will be allowed to take the just man's life—in the most painful and shameful way possible even—and then what? (See, he stands fast.) Job considers this much later: and though worms destroy this body, "yet in my flesh shall I see God" (19:26)—see, he stands fast. And so one might be persuaded to think that the third and final act of this unfin-

[7] Ibid.

ished fairy-tale drama might seal, from man's side, a new covenant between man and God, one not based on the law of justice and retribution, but on love. In that final act God will allow the adversary even to take the just man's life. Perhaps he will allow it over and over and over again, until the last of the just are expunged from the face of the earth. And when the day comes for all the heavenly beings to appear again before the Lord, the adversary will come also, and present—himself; he will have no further explanations to offer. There will be nothing else to turn to. There will be no stone to turn—except one. On that day the adversary will have to admit that there is no one so faithful as Job and the fairy tale story will suddenly reveal itself as having been not about Job and not about Job's testing, but about God's love and patience even with the most wayward of His sons, a love and patience in whose passionate action some, perhaps hosts, even millions of His other sons are allowed to participate. Such are the just who suffer.

Thus does Job piece up in himself and in time what is lacking in the salvific work of the God who transcends time. For Job willed to be grateful to God in good times and in bad, in sickness and in health, until even the most wayward can do nothing but notice the single task of all the heavenly beings—even those lowly ones on earth. And if even those sons made of mortal earth can do it, even those who suffer like the upright Job, what makes it so difficult for you? There is no one left to test; the man's love has exceeded the power of his natural life. It is impossible, and just for that reason it is now noticeable: See, he stands. In fact, now it *must* be noticed; it cannot be avoided or forgotten. The impossible has been achieved—by a man. God, who was willing to bet on the man, has won. And Job and

Job's children have had their part in His victory. To be part of such…

Muß es sein? Es muß sein.[8] Must it be this way? Must it be suffered blindly and without knowledge, as it is here, as Job himself suffers without knowing the purposes of heaven? If it were possible to volunteer for this position, who could dare it? For might not the volunteer be motivated by pride, or by the desire to prove or repay or justify? Would not knowledge, here, engender *hubris*? Elie Wiesel says, "this is probably the most subtle [of all the injustices done to Job]: *he never learns the full truth*."[9] But, first, this injustice is universal, for none of us ever learns the full extent of his own story (and in this we might be grateful too); and second, it is only because of Job's lack of knowledge that we can see the extremity of his heroism: the *nothing* which causes his love. Job does not volunteer for suffering for the glory of God; it is brought upon him, and it is terrible. So terrible that a part of him wishes to revolt. He does not know anything of what it may be worth, and the story does not say his suffering is redemptive, that the adversary (for example) gives up or breaks down or weeps in recognition of his willful heartlessness. But look, Job answers it; and he answers it even though that very part of him which is his wife suggests that he turn his back and leave life cursing God. He will not let go of God or righteousness though he has no cause, no reason, no capacity to guess why he should hang on, or even how he can hang on. Perhaps we should

---

[8] These two phrases are written under the opening chords of the first *grave* and first *allegro* of the final movement of Beethoven's last string quartet, number 16.

[9] Wiesel, "Job," 127.

read that little interchange between man and wife as the dialogue of the just man's soul with his mind, and his soul refuses to let go of living before God. For much of life it may well be that the mind suffices to lead the soul in the right way—for the world, too, is a book in which we read of God, but here the soul reaches out where the mind sees nothing, and the nothing is palpable and darkness, and in the face of that darkness the mind desires to revolt.[10] And that revolt might even be... expected, expected of—whom, exactly? What kind of mind and will, to be precise?

⊕

Tarry spirit; whither wander you? There are no further excuses, no available explanations, no further experimental variables and no further subjects for the adversary to place between himself and the face of God. No wonder there is no story of the satan returning. God's will throughout the story is that the adversary accept the love of God, see his own error, the poverty of his power against love, and the perversity of his proceeding against it. When the adversary sees this (which he will see only when there is nothing else left to see—when the world is a barren wasteland and he alone is returned to tell) he will, of his own free will, turn back from roaming the face of the earth.—Or he will not turn back at all, ever. He can wish Job had never existed, but now wherever in the abyss he roams he *knows* otherwise, and this knowledge is a sign not only of his failure, but of his self-delusion. There could not be, according to

[10] A whole philosophy invents itself here, as in Albert Camus's *The Rebel*; its figure might be Camus's Dr Rieux, in *The Plague*, or Ivan Karamazov.

him, a love that was for nothing; but Job now shows, with nothing and for nothing, that he will not abandon God. And knowledge of a delusion destroys it, and the truth sets free a cry of gratitude. And on that day all the heavenly beings will appear again before the Lord, and present themselves before his face.—Or not. Wrapped in its own will, may not a spiritual being hang on to its delusion even in the face of knowledge that it is delusion?

⊕

But the fairy tale of Job does not continue as this fairy tale I have outlined or in the manner we might expect. At least it does not continue so in the book of *Job*. After Job refuses his wife's counsel, three of his friends appear from distant lands; they will counsel him further. They have heard of his sudden trials and have come to give him… comfort. Seeing his sorrow they weep; they tear their cloaks and sit in silence for seven days and seven nights. All the signs of Job's life repeat themselves. It is as if each day of creation, each act of God those days described, even the day sanctified by God's rest for praise, each of the days Job had handed over to his sons for their liturgy, has now within it some element over which good men must sorrow. And so they do. It is as if all of creation, in each of its days, groans, here, with Job, on his dungheap, and speaks not.

And the prose narrative comes to an end without coming to a conclusion; the folk-tale storytelling is replaced by theological discussion, which, so very strangely, is in verse. The counterpointing narratives of country heaven disappear, and we hear the playing out of an entirely earthly drama, but now a drama of argument, not action, a setting out of *logos*, not *mythos*. And the logos works only from the side of Job and his friends. And for a long time there is no Logos from heaven. What the comforters offer is bare argument, barren science; as if they were deriving a general solution to the problem of a quadratic equation. This barrenness will be, in fact, a great deal of the problem, perhaps the root of the matter, for Job. For Job becomes offended; but that is to come.

"And Job's friends sat with him on the ground for seven days and seven nights, and no one spoke a word to him, for they saw that his suffering was very great" (2:13). This is a good start; for his friends come just to be with him, and they remain, sharing in his grief and suffering. In silence, for seven days.

JOB 3

Job Opens His Mouth

"After this Job opened his mouth. . ."[1]

That Job's friends are silent for so long, that they sit with him in dust and ashes, having wept and rent their garments, shows that they are, indeed, Job's friends. Only love can be silent for so long in such an intimate nearness. This is the last element of the folk tale: the long silence of the comforters of Job. It is the deep humanness of this silence, its

---

[1] In a footnote to his monograph *On Job: God-talk and the Suffering of the Innocent* (Maryknoll, NY: Orbis, 1987), Gustavo Gutierrez claims that Aquinas, among others, seeks to "moderate the tone of Job's protests" (110 n1). I do not find this to be an accurate representation of what St Thomas is doing. Job's cursing (*maledicere*), Thomas says, "is nothing else but speaking evil (*malum dicere*)," which can be done in three ways—causing evil, as in a judge's condemnation; calling down evil (as in our usual sense of "curse"); or disclosing an evil of the past, present, or future. Job is clearly doing the last, revealing how evil that day really was which came disguised as a blessing—the day of his birth (cf. Aquinas, *Literal Exposition*, 100). That it is natural for a sufferer to complain, that no one would choose a life of ceaseless dying, as Gutierrez, quoting Fray Louis de León, affirms (110 n1), Aquinas too says. E.g.: "For reason cannot remove the condition of nature. Now it is natural to the sensual nature that it be delighted and rejoice in fitting things and be pained and saddened over harmful things" (*Literal Exposition*, 99). "For even if life itself is desirable, a life subject to misery is not" (105). "[Job shows] that it would have been useless—no, harmful rather—for him to have been kept alive" (106).

42

unspeakable and so unspoken love, its very distance from poetry and speech that perhaps invited the later writer—if there was a later writer[2]—to insert the speeches that follow, and to know it was necessary to shape them into poetry. It is because he listened to—and in—this silence that he could write. Just so, it is because of their love, the perfect silent presence of his friends for so long, that Job, after seven days, feels able to speak. After such silence words would have a new weight, a heft of which our constant busy speech is unaware.[3]

It is generally accepted among scholars that the book of *Job* has been edited or redacted here; that at this point an old folk tale and a new problematic are joined. And it is generally thought that there are some imperfections in this redaction, that, for instance, the character of Job in the two stories is considerably different; they do not fit together; they are not the same man. But without attempting to guess at the various times and purposes or sources of redaction (about which there might be everlasting, if not eternal, disagreement), let us note that the book as we see it here—

---

[2] I mean here not to call into question the scholarly consensus that the authors of the folk tale and the poetic speeches are distinct, and separated in time and place by an unknown distance—even though such arguments usually follow upon changes of style and presume an inspired author would not change his speech pattern radically mid-story. I merely request the reader to keep in mind that insofar as revelation is inspired by God there is no later writer. Aquinas, following Jerome, notes the change to hexameter poetry and considers that this allows more heightened language than our everyday complaints (*Literal Exposition*, 102).

[3] If one is going to read the larger portion of *Job* as the revelation that Job has been the victim of his people, as does Girard, one has to break the book after this silence of the friends, rather than at the end of chapter two. He is not that victim here—yet.

breaking from folk tale to speeches of complaint and response, indictment and defense, speeches of lawyerly complexity in some of the Bible's most powerful poetry— this redactive breaking and joining, this cutting and pasting of disparate parts, which makes both the folk tale and the speeches (were each considered separately) into something different, has a mimetic counterpart: it is a lot like life. The fairy tale of childhood (however difficult or happy) is broken by a dawn of rational self-consideration and consideration of the world; the speechless infant learns to speak and later—as the world breaks in—to argue, to bless or curse; but the infant, the young child, and the embittered or saintly man are all somehow "redacted." They are all joined—however diverse their spirits—into the one person's life. We become ourselves; in doing so we join wildly different styles of life—who would believe it is the same person? So, too, with the Book of Job as it has come down to us. The whole has become *Job*. Many such redactions, as we look at our own life, are surprising or troubling. Some are as surprising and troubling as Job's redaction here when he opens his mouth and curses the day of his birth, like Prometheus on his rock, Oedipus at his self-discovery, or Lear's "let chaos come again"—"for why is light given to a man whose way is hidden and hemmed in by God?" (3:23).

As many readers in many generations have considered, the change in Job here does seem to be a change in character, for the patient Job had said to his wife, "shall we receive good at the hand of God, and shall we not receive evil?" (2:10)—a sentence which also, let it be noted, confesses to being hemmed in by God. But *that* Job did not complain. The earlier Job seems to admit that a man does not *know* the way he will travel, but faith in God only requires that each step be taken with gratitude and justice, and where the path goes is entrusted to the maker of paths—the Lord who gives and takes away.

But here Job curses the very entrance to the path of his life, that path which, it now seems, tempted him forward by joy only to abandon him in the barren waste, more horrible than the grave, which Job now discovers his life to be. The satan has gotten under his skin, and Job wishes he himself had never been put into that skin. He wishes to reverse the command of creation—"that day, let it be darkness" (3:4)—and he is become, it seems, "bitter in soul" (3:20). He wishes to uncreate the day of his birth and the night of his conception, to make them disappear from the calendar of days. His life is more horrible than the grave, because here his hopes are mocked—"what I fear comes upon me, and what I dread befalls" (3:25); in the grave it may turn out that the king has only rebuilt ruins for himself—for his city falls again after him, but the ruin of the kingdom is not then the king's concern, and in the grave even the wicked cease from trouble, and the weary rest, and the slave is free of his master. But Job, above ground and lost, has no such ease. Nor is there ease forthcoming; he hopes for it, and it comes not. He has no rest, but trouble comes:

> I am not at ease, nor am I quiet;
> I have no rest, but trouble comes. (3:26)

It seems his cursing of life is complete. Though he has not cursed God directly, he has made a long and heartfelt incantation to revoke one of His works. But if we listen closely to his execrations (3–10) and the lament he breaks down into thereafter (11–26), then, just here in the last line of his complaint, we can hear the undertone which connects the complaining Job with the earlier, more openly sublime character, steadfast in his refusal to curse. Job wishes for ease, for rest, not for death. Or he imagines even death as allowing an activity—rest, surcease of sorrow. Or, more accurately, he imagines death as encompassing the dissolution of earthly passions—those of princes, of the wicked, of prisoners and slaves all equally—but this dissolution of passion is an experience of the living soul: it is experienced as rest. Death is attractive because it offers a calmness of life for the soul; and for this rest we hear not only Job's hope, but his heartfelt gratitude, which he imagines as the gratitude a prisoner and a slave would feel upon their release, or a king unburdened of his majesty, and so in his desire for rest we hear his desire, still, to be grateful even to the God who has hedged his way. To rest in gratitude for rest. For where could the just and perfect man rest but in gratitude? Job wishes to be relieved because in his constant pain and physical and emotional torment he is pulled away from the act which gives meaning to life: gratitude, in the liturgies of which he had brought up his children. The life for which, until now, he had always been able to bless God now eludes him in the constant pain of his body and mind. He seems now hemmed in, not just by God but from God, hemmed in in such a way that he feels God is unavailable. He would rejoice exultingly (3:22) in death because he thinks that his path, and God's making of it, would no longer be hidden from him, as it now is. Death would be God's coming to him again, or at least rest from this absence.

Job does not, like Lear, wish chaos to come again or the seeds of nature to be crushed; even at the highest rhetorical point of his complaint he does not carry himself off to that. He does not curse God; he does not condemn the world;

he does not even repent his daily ineffectual (it now seems) sacrifices; he does not renounce gratitude or call praise foolishness. He does not choose not to be—even if he wishes for it. He finds himself incapable of gratitude or praise or the vision of what God is up to in his life, but *he wishes it not to be so*; he wishes to be thankful, in rest, for rest. He damns the day of his birth *because* were he stillborn he "would now be lying quiet" (3:13). He wishes for that good he knows everyone from prince to slave is grateful for. Beneath his complaint it is almost possible to hear another less ancient prayer: "Eternal rest grant unto me, O Lord; *et lux perpetua luceat me.*" This is not a curse of God. It is a wish for a superior light than that of day.

Job does not believe that the hedging of fate which afflicts him is good, that sorrow is good, that his suffering is spiritually helpful—if he does so believe, he certainly does not say so here—but he does, in the face of his most terrible affliction, wish to be grateful. The character of the original Job, the one who blessed God to his face upon the death of all his household and the loss of all his property, is not completely defaced by the onslaughts of the adversary. He had trained himself in thankfulness, and by so constant an awareness of God's presence brought up in himself the desire to give thanks constantly, a desire which hides even here in his curse of himself, even here among these rocks. We see in the oft-supposed changed Job the heart of the same Job like whom there is no one upon the earth: the Job who rises early in gratitude.

There is a story Elie Wiesel tells[4] of an evening in Aus-

---

[4] See the introduction by Robert McAfee Brown in Elie Wiesel, *The Trial of God*, vii.

chwitz whose point, I think, is the same as this. Wiesel tells of three rabbis who one night in the camp bring God to trial for the torture and death of his children. At the trial no one spoke on God's behalf, and, in conclusion, He was convicted. The child Elie feels like weeping, but he does not weep. Then the rabbis became aware of the time, that it was the time for the evening prayer; and so they began to pray. The rabbis wished to rest in understanding, but understanding was not granted them. Their trial and condemnation was an expression of this desire to rest in understanding; their condemnation, then, arose from the same source as their prayer—the desire for an understanding with God. And turning from condemnation to prayer does not turn their passion—for the tap-root of both acts is the same. So, too, with Job's curse, which is a curse not of God, but of his life's path, which has taken him to where he feels incapable.

And here, perhaps, another psychological truth becomes visible: it is not possible to lament except in the presence of love and out of love. Love is the deep well from which arises Job's complaint, as with the laments of Jeremiah and some of the psalms. A Stoic does not lament because the part of him that is divine is his reason: it is part of and returns to the eternal fire, and the weeping part, the part of passion, is merely animal. But the Judeo-Christian story is that the particular person, which is more than the function of reason, is the created image of God: the creature comes to life because of God's breath. And praise is only possible for—and is the proper act of—this finite, rational, breathing creature. It is possible—because the creature is finite and must breathe—for our kind of creature to be oppressed by evil, suffering, and pain, for breathing to be torturously difficult, and it is possible that under such pressure the creature may deny, or forget, or abandon, or wish to abandon its function—God knows (as do I and every other sinner) it has been done under considerably less constraining circumstances—but such apostasy is not necessary. Under the pressure of such evils and the constant distraction of pain that song of praise which is always the proper function of man expresses itself as lamentation. Job laments. Perhaps, in fact, being silent—like a Stoic—under the pressure of such adversity is a sign that the adversary has won, but the Phalarian bull which the world has become to Job has not stopped his mouth, though it may force his music into a different key.

JOB 4–5

Eliphaz Speaks

THE DEPTH OF JOB'S LAMENT requires a response, but what verbal response can be given to such a curse and lament? The only thing that could really satisfy Job is the presence of the one by whom Job feels abandoned. Eliphaz wonders if he should speak. "If one dared a word, could you bear it?" He apparently knows that, to one suffering, the words of a comforter can be like the scratch of cloth on a burn, or the pressure of a finger on a bone-deep bruise. Eliphaz begins carefully; he remembers that in other days Job had instructed many, given strength to the feeble, support to the stumbling. Other sufferers had come to Job and his words had been as medicine to their diseases. "But now it is come to you, and you are impatient; it touches you, and you are dismayed" (4:5). Though he does not know it, Eliphaz here points out that what the adversary wanted has come to pass; he touches Job's flesh, not someone else's.

Suppose that it is so, suppose it is easy to teach about suffering from the early position of Job, when things are going well, but less easy to teach when one is oneself in suffering's classroom, when one is oneself the lesson of the day. And the lesson of the night. For all the world to look at. And there is no release. But then, what is one's teaching worth if it does not come from one's bones? and how could it have been medicinal to those Job must have cared for and spo-

50

ken to if it were not as true as blood? A problem underlies his speech, for Eliphaz attests that Job's touch was not painful to the distraught, and then, perhaps, says to Job what Job had said to the sufferer he touched, the one whose wounds he dressed: "Is not your piety your assurance, and the integrity of your ways your hope?" (4:6).

Now let us step back and imagine Job saying this in his earlier days. Indeed, who could say this but someone like Job, someone whose piety is constant, whose integrity is so far from shaken that he cannot imagine impiety, the very idea must be suggested to him from outside—"Why don't you curse God and die?"—but even then it is hardly understood—"What? shall we accept good from the Lord and not also accept evil?" So perhaps Eliphaz is reminding Job of his own words and that he should be comforted in his integrity. But the same sentence may not be the same sentence when it is spoken by different people; whether it is medicinal or poisonous depends on the doctor—and the patient.

How did those words work on the suffering ones Job had come across? Could someone who heard them from Job but had, till the trial came upon him, put his hope in his wealth, wit, talent, youth, or strength—could that one be hurt by Job's medicine: "Is not your piety your assurance, and the integrity of your ways your hope?" Or would not the calmness of his utterance, its glorious assumption of the good, and presumption of the integrity of the person to whom he speaks, coupled with Job's obvious goodness—for he is binding up the wounds of this injured one he does not know—would this not begin the sloughing off of the old and now brutalized flesh of faith in one's self and begin a revitalization of a better faith and hope: to have such integrity? Would not that itself be real health, and now, as one sees and desires it, the bones grow stronger and straighter, one's skin and musculature more supple and fresh. Thus the suffering becomes one of rebirth, and the healing a better birth, a birth to knowledge and love of the giver, to the assurance of the permanent presence of God, an assurance for which piety is not a cloak or some practice of an additional virtue, but wells up from the center of one's being, from which everything one is grows. This sentence—"is not your piety your assurance?"—can be accepted by the workaday sinner from the just man, for from him it is as if the sun breaks through a lifetime's overcast. After such a word the sick one knows where to place his hope, though he had not before—or knowing, had not done so before. And hearing it from such a one, we wish to place our hope where he assumes it already is: in piety and integrity. This becomes our firmer purpose. The destruction of his surrounding goods makes this easier for the one to whom those goods had been too much a concern. It is easier now to see heaven, for there is no roof in the way.

Or to someone just a bit less perfect than Job, someone only occasionally forgetful or inadequate, or backhandedly cruel—would these words—"is not your piety your assurance, and the integrity of your ways your hope?"—far from prodding his pain, not set him thinking of his own unpunctual gratitude, the fitful nature of his integrity? And then the assurance of this bruising reminder is that one might die as one occasionally lives, outside of the presence of God: the tent cord pulled up without wisdom (4:21). And for this timely reminder would he not give thanks even in the tent of suffering? And *for* the tent of suffering?

But it is not clear that either of these situations, one or the other of which applies to most mortals, applies to Job, like whom there is no one upon the earth: righteous and God-fearing, awakening early to gratitude. Nor has Eliphaz been affirmed as a proper speaker of Job's healing word. What could such a remark—"is not your piety your assurance and the integrity of your ways your hope?"—mean *to Job*, whose self-understanding—one shared with God, as we know—is of his perfection in piety? What is it that Job's piety could give assurance of? It *cannot* be what Eliphaz says next, for when he asks Job to consider "what innocent perishes, since when are the upright destroyed?" (4:7), Job must be shocked. He must be shocked because he is sitting right next to Eliphaz and it seems that Eliphaz does not see that Job's setbacks are not merely material setbacks, nor do they appear at all temporary. Nor, most importantly, is he seeing Job. *In himself Job knows* the upright being destroyed and the innocent perishing. Eliphaz seems either not to understand the destructiveness Job has suffered or to be implying that Job must be among those who plowed mischief and sowed trouble (4:9). In any case, he cannot be looking at Job as he asks his question (4:7), or, if looking, he cannot see.

Perhaps, glancing at Job as he asks this, he all but sees the perishing innocent, and then he looks quickly away—to those who plow evil and sow trouble, to the lions among men, the rapacious and violent (4:8–11). He looks everywhere save at Job—the innocent, the righteous, he whom there is no one like upon the earth. And then, in a pause of this avoidance—which is his avoidance of Job—he speaks of a nightmare, a terrifying trance, a breath across his face and a shape passing before his eyes (4:12–17). Is it an

ecstatic encounter with God, or as close as any of the comforters will get to seeing Job? The passage in Hebrew is
uncanny; and its uncanniness is exact. For this nightmarish
terror—an innocent perishing—which makes Eliphaz's hair
start up in dread seems to be sitting next to him, or across
from him in the circle: A word is brought to him, and he
hears a whisper of it (4:12).

His own word still hangs in the air: "Is not your piety
your assurance?" He hears it again, but the words now seem
to be referring to this living sore, to be emanating from this
leaking pus-bag, and quickly he shakes his head to recover
and seems to hear, "can a mortal be just before God? a man
upright before his maker?" (4:17). Could he, Eliphaz, hold
his own piety an assurance? Could any of us? What passing
shape first offered this suggestion—piety is assurance—to
Eliphaz? For Eliphaz himself is not the one whom there is
no one like upon the earth. How, from him, can these
words come? What passes between him and Job? Was that
shape one of the darker sons of heaven? And this further
question—"can a mortal be just?"—who spoke it? Where is
the fog creature here?—Which? Eliphaz shakes his head to
recover.

Between these two sentences he (like, apparently, the
original Hebrew) loses his bearings: "Is not your piety your
assurance?" "Can a mortal be just before God?" Does he
wake or dream? Or does something far greater than a
dream interpose itself: "Can a man be righteous before
God? A mortal blameless against his Maker?" Or is he waking to the nightmare? If the first question can be answered
positively, then the second must be answerable in the same
way and with that same pious gratitude Job has always
exhibited. And if the second is answered negatively, as Eli-

phaz seems to require, then how could the first ever be true? In which case, what shall we say of perishing? Eliphaz is made dizzy by this whisper, he has lost his footing. And in his terror he is unable to see *Job*—that mortal who is just before God. Eliphaz seems afraid a judgment has been spoken, even from his own mouth. He stumbles, he speaks generalizations, like a suddenly blind man feeling for where the wall usually is. Through the whole next chapter he gropes nervously for the usual handholds—the fool is abandoned (5:2–5), the clever are trapped in their contrivance (5:12–15), and between them man is born for trouble as the sparks fly upward (5:7). And he advises:

> As for me, I would seek God
> and to Him commit my cause. (5:8)

All these lines may be true of us, good advice *for us*; any of them may be adequate for our own explanation, but Job is neither foolish nor clever; he is innocent; he is righteous and destroyed. There is none like him on the earth. Eliphaz's speech does not touch Job. Job has never ceased to commit his cause to God. To whom is Eliphaz speaking?

To be more exacting: Eliphaz is caught in a dilemma, and he is just on the verge of seeing it, which would be seeing Job, for Job is the living dilemma. On the one side is Eliphaz's traditional belief that piety and integrity are loved by God and holding to them is holding to God who is the ground of justice as well as hope: piety is assurance. For Eliphaz, this assurance will be visible in worldly protection and success. Losing such success is a sign of impiety. On the other side is the whispered question "can a man be righteous before God?," from which follows the louder answer that God does not even ascribe such glory to his angels

(4:18). This, too, seems to be true, but it destroys the hope which piety and justice guaranteed on the first side. Additionally, that first side has been belied, in Job's case, by God Himself, who affirmed Job's perfection. This perfection Job has illustrated to us as gratitude. Suppose we had been justified by God Himself—then would not our piety be our assurance? Would it not be ungrateful (at the least) to think and live otherwise? So perhaps the voice Eliphaz hears in this little wind is demonic, for it tempts to despair. Eliphaz reacts as if he feels so, for he runs away from the question that uncanny voice raises, back to the traditional wisdom of God's obvious justice and so the educative, rectificatory, or retributive interpretation of suffering: "Man begets mischief" (5:7), "God wounds, but he binds up" (5:8). But these cannot be true of Job's suffering given God's praise of him. We have heard the divine affirmation: Job is just before God.

So we are left with the terror on the other side of the dilemma, that the voice whispering in the wind to Eliphaz is the same voice that will return at the end of the book: the voice of the all-holy. But if no one is righteous before God, or no one except Job, or if before our Maker we are always in the wrong, then this voice seems to be destroying the connections between justice, piety, and assurance, as well as all human grounds for hope. If no one can be there—just—before God, then what is the use of trying to be just? And if no one can be there, then there is no ground for hope in God's favor, no connection between piety and assurance. Well, perhaps we should try to be just, and thus get as close as we can to holiness. Eliphaz might be moving in this direction in the last half of chapter five. It is an educative view of suffering, a comfort and hope that for the best of us might be sufficient:

> Happy the man whom God corrects,
> spurn not the discipline of the Lord;
> for He makes a bruise, but He dresses it;
> He wounds, but by His hand we are healed.
> (5:17–18)

And Eliphaz, *we* may agree, is correct:

> We have tried this and it is true;
> hear it and know it yourself. (5:27)

But does this comfort find *Job*? See *him*? Touch *him*? Does *Job* need correction? Eliphaz is presuming he does. Can this be true? Even if true, could it be Eliphaz's place to teach this to him like whom there is no one else upon the earth? Can this be the work of a comforter? Does he speak rightly *to Job*? This educative splitting of the difference between the sides of the dilemma fits *me*—indeed, any reasonable sinner can admit that correction by the omniscient and omnipotent Lord must be salutary and fruitful—but what can need correction in Job? Further, can the wisdom of those whose house is of clay speak truly to the one who lives in the house of God? Or is this whole chapter like the blurred speech of the nightmare mumbling its terror into the ears of one already awake?

Eliphaz's speech, like several to come, *can* be of comfort, but not under the condition that it is in Eliphaz's mouth, nor that it is given to Job. However, even for Job himself and in Job himself Eliphaz inadvertently speaks the truth:

> He will deliver you from six troubles;
> in seven no evil shall touch you.

In famine He will redeem you from death,
in war from the power of the sword. . . .
At destruction and famine you shall laugh,
and shall not fear the beasts of the earth.
For you shall be in league with the stones of the field
and the beasts of the field shall be at peace with you.
You shall know that your tent is safe,
you shall inspect your fold and miss nothing.
(5:19–24)

This speech is true in that in all his troubles the evil has not settled in Job's soul; in a famine of all earthly goods, Job has not suffered the spiritual death which would have been confessed in cursing God. In four messengers and three friends this evil—the evil—has not touched him. As the stones and beasts always fulfill their function as stone or beast, Job still fulfills his function as a man—to stand in the presence of God. In this he is a rock; he is in league with the stones in the constancy of their praise.

This realization allows us a better solution of the dilemma. To the whispered question "who can be just before God?" the answer should be, "the one who lives from the experience that it is not he who holds to justice, but God who, because of his constant presence, enables the just man to stand justly." The one who is constantly in God's presence, and does not wander here and there. It is, in that case, no mere creature of dust who stands before God, but one in whose being God participates and who is therefore and thereby just, who stands there. We stand before God insofar as we participate in God, and this participation is justice and piety. Our justice and piety are the measure of the extent to which we allow God to stand in us. So it is not on one's own justice or integrity that one depends (as the first part of the dilemma seemed to say) but on the integrity of God, in which the person participates, granting him integrity. Such integrity is above our power to attain of ourselves, but it is in our power to turn away from this—as those who sow trouble do. So we may hold both that "no one (of himself) is just before God" and "in our piety is our assurance." What this piety is is God working through us. At this Job is perfect. This is how his life is both pious and just, and so also an assurance.

So Eliphaz makes two errors in speaking to Job. He talks of justice and integrity literally or simply—as an accident of being belonging to God or to a man, not as something which is God and in which we participate—or not. He presumes thereby that Job's deepest complaint is about the visible suffering, not about the way this constant suffering reduces to all but nothing his ability to be aware of the presence of God—in which is his integrity. Secondly, presuming the simple and literal "equal weights" view of the good man and his happiness, and noting the latter is manifestly lacking in Job's physical life, he implies (though he does not say) that the opposite conclusion must be true of Job—he is not a good man.

The premises sound vaguely familiar: Eliphaz's simple and empirical interpretation of justice and its rewards (the good are good and are given good; the bad are not good and are corrected by punishment) is simply the obverse of the satan's earlier question: does Job fear God for nought?[1] Satan, too, expects every relation to be measurable in scales;

---

[1] This relation to the satan on the part of the friends is something Wiesel points out as well: "There are three terms, in Hebrew, to describe a friend: *Yadid, Khaver,* and *Rea. Yadid* means: *Yad* and *yad*—hand in

economy measures all. And the conclusion, or rather fundamental principle, of both stories—the satan's and Eliphaz's—is the same: man is at best a trainable Id under the reality principle of the supposed divine justice: to receive good, do good. Were this traditional view true it would follow of necessity that love does not exist; and fear of the Lord is merely *Realpolitik*—when paid it produces peace, as the world understands it.

hand. *Rea—resh-ayin*—is close to *ra*: evil. . . . They were Satan's friends. For they did to Job psychologically, mentally, what Satan had done physically" ("Job," 124). This nearness of the friends to Satan—they seem almost to participate in his being, and dizzyingly lose their footing—can also be understood anthropologically as the spirit or infectious force of mimetic competition in which Job resists being submersed, which is Girard's point. Girard, however, does not attend to the first two chapters of *Job*, thinking it offers a metaphysical rather than a moral and anthropological consideration of the problem of evil.

JOB 6-7
Job's Answer

THE SPEECH OF ELIPHAZ is like the drop of water that supersaturates the sand of Job's life; now, when weighed in the balance, Job's calamities and afflictions are heavier than the sand of the sea (6:3). His troubles have been deep, but now, in his time of need and hunger for support, his friend feeds him egg white, raw (6:6). Eliphaz probably does not even know that is what he is doing, but Job, having expected real food from his friend, is disgusted; for while the arrows of the Almighty are in him his friend talks in the generalities of philosophy about the happiness of those reproved by God, and the healing stripes of punishment for those who require reform. Honest words would be of force, but what in his friend's reproof touches Job? Thus, this food is loathsome to him. He might have said, "you know not me." In fact, he asks his friends to look him in the face and see if he is lying (6:28). Job's despair is now complete, for he is not merely abandoned, but his friends feed him poison. He turns himself entirely over to God for destruction:

> O that I might have my request...
> that it would please God to crush me,
> that He would let loose His hand and cut me off.
> This would be my consolation;

On *Job*

I would exult even in pain unsparing
For I have not denied the words of the Holy One.
(6:8–10)

Though Eliphaz does not understand him, indeed over-
burdens his suffering with his attempt at comfort, Job still
trusts that God knows not so much his suffering as his
integrity. Filled with despair of the world, Job says he
would exult in fulfilling God's command to die. This cry of
Job's is, then, of a piece with his response to his first
friend—his wife: he has not denied and will not deny the
words of the Holy One. Some scholars suggest that this
first line may be sarcastic, something more like, "I would be
happy if God would show how holy He is by killing me
openly." This interpretation would make the Job of the
speeches a different character from the Job of the folk tale.
But even so, it is interesting that in such a despairing prayer
Job still speaks a hidden truth. He imagines God's hand is
held back, that it is not free to cut him off. A cynic might
say that God does not cut him off because, if He did, He
could not see how the bet turns out, but the truth of the
story is that it was God's love for Job that set the bounds on
the adversary's freedom. God has not decreed Job's death,
certainly not his spiritual death—which would come by
cursing God—or indeed any of the evils that have befallen
him; He has decreed a limited power to the freedom of the
satan. And the adversary is not free to cut him off from the
source of life, God would have to do that himself; and if He
would so order, Job would, exulting, embrace it. By confessing *this* Job has not denied the words of the Holy One.
Rather, Job is himself, already in this prayer, the living
exultant witness he imagines that death would make him.
If Job knew the story he was in, he would also be exultant,

for even in the pain unsparing which he is suffering he has not denied the words of the Holy One. Though God does not speak or directly answer Job's prayer, still, it is He to whom Job holds fast, He in whose decrees Job places trust, for the speech of Eliphaz has driven home to Job that

> In truth I have no help in me,
> and any resource is driven from me. (6:13)

Knowing his own lack of resource, Job hopes that what is to be done will be done quickly.

Job is made neither of bronze nor of stone (6:12); he cannot help himself, and his friend—far from being a source of consolation—has, by his speech, redoubled the burden. Such a friend is like a stream one noted in passing during winter, banks covered with ice, but when the caravan turns from its course in summer to look for it, it perishes; for the need it had hoped to satisfy by the banks of the stream found only a dry, empty gully (6:15-20). Job makes it clear that his disappointment is not material or physical; he has not asked his friends for ransom or sacrifices from their wealth. He wishes not for explanation but for someone to share in his abandonment; such communion is the water he seeks. In failing to see to whom he speaks about the moral significance of suffering, and in treating its truth as merely about physical life, Eliphaz's words of comfort are worse than useless. Job, like whom there is no one upon the earth, cannot be corrected by punishment, for he needs no correction. Since Eliphaz does not see this, he has no communion with Job. That Eliphaz considers God's saving as economic is a further confession of lack of communion; Eliphaz's understanding of the divine disallows his participation in the divine life which is required for any true communion between human beings. Eliphaz's words are a danger—a temptation to despair. His words reduce the relation to God to economy and prudence, and so make of Job's heretofore just life's ineffectiveness at producing safety an argument against its being just; they reduce his daily liturgy to utility, and reduce joy to enjoyment. But things were never thus for Job, and suffering does not change the truth of things.

Job's cry indicates that he hears Eliphaz precisely as this temptation to despair, and this implies Job's recognition that someone whose hope is limited to the world is already in despair, for in the physical world Job has nothing. Job is being driven to a supersaturated despair by Eliphaz because he had expected the spiritual good of communal understanding and compassion, and finds this, on top of everything else, is also absent. The misunderstanding adds weight to Job's burden. Job knows that hope for the good is not limited to the material world; he has not spent his life attempting to hold fast to some thing, but to gratitude, piety, and justice. He has no thing; he needs the real food of communion; only that could be consolation. Eliphaz brings an overweight of sea-sand. It is as if the speech of Eliphaz has revealed not only that he and Job are not friends at all, but that they could not have ever been friends, for not only does Eliphaz presume against Job's virtue in his philosophizing, but he also attempts to teach him without knowing who he is—one who really does put his trust in the decrees of the Holy One, not in the Holy One's material rewards. How can someone who is truly a friend be in this position?

Job begs him,

> But now be pleased to look at me
> for I will not lie to your face. (6:28)

But could Eliphaz bear it now? to look at Job in the face, whom he has presumed against?

> Turn, I pray, let no wrong be done;
> turn now, my vindication is at stake. (6:29)

We must suppose that Eliphaz, who has traveled so far, who is himself concerned to be righteous before God, who could sit silently for seven days and seven nights with his afflicted friend, hears Job breaking in this plea, and out of his own love for justice and perhaps even in half-recognized submission to a punishment he deserves at the hand of friendship, he turns to look at Job in the face, and Job asks him:

> Is there wrong on my tongue,
> cannot my taste discern calamity? (6:30)

Humbled, Eliphaz lowers his head, and Job teaches him the wisdom he has learned in his suffering. It is at once more personal than Eliphaz's speech, it is about himself—"I am allotted," "I am full of tossing," "my flesh," "my skin," "my days"; and it is also more concrete—"slave," "unpaid hireling," "months of misery," "troubled nights," "clothed with worms and dirt," "scabbed," "breaking afresh"—no metaphors of grain, or tents, or fires whose sparks fly upward, but exactly what Eliphaz sees looking at the face of Job—to the maggot. It is a philosophy that starts in the ashes Job sits in, a wisdom his body groans forth from the gate to Sheol. Job speaks the philosophy of his flesh.

And then, his friend being incapable of a living philosophy or any comfort or sustenance, Job turns to his only possible upholder, the invisible presence before whom he has lived. First addressing God like a lover whom he feels is turning away, Job begs,

Remember that my life is like the wind,
I shall not look on happiness again. (7:7)

And then, unanswered, he continues in the full cry of despair:

Therefore I will not restrain my mouth.
I will speak in the anguish of my spirit. (7:11)
...
What is a man that You exalt him,
or pay him any heed?
You inspect him every morning,
and test him at every moment.
How long will You not look away,
nor let me alone to swallow my spit? (7:17–19)

If Job sins, if we sin, can our sins harm God? Then why does He concern Himself? Why watch so intimately? So closely that even our spit may testify against us. Can He not let us be? If we sin, can He not forgive us? For soon we will be dust and He will look upon us no more. Even as He watches we disappear. What is it to Him? What matter that He sifts us so? Watching even as we spit. That example shows how absolutely Job has lived in the face of God. He has not been seeking entertainments, practicing the absence of God; far from it; he is aware of the presence of the Holy One even to his smallest act.

Should we answer Job's question? Dare we even think about these questions with the concreteness Job gives them? Why, how can we matter so much? Because that's what love for a person means: everything counts. Everything about the beloved matters utterly. That is what the permanent presence of God means. Who can live with it? Who could consciously bear such love? Would we rather be like Job's brothers, "who have passed me by like a brook" (6:15), the happy brook in the valley of the world? But then, like the water in the heat of summer, "they flow and then cease to be; in the heat they disappear" (6:17). And so would we be if we imagined we had help in ourselves, the strength of stones (6:12–13); whole caravans of human beings are so, turning from the path and perishing (6:18–20)—and this is what his friend's speech would have him come to be: "thus you have become for me" (6:21).

⊕

Job seems here to wish to suppose the physical world enough, he seems to reduce himself almost... almost to wishing just for the animal comforts of sleep (7:13), a brief housing against the weather (7:10), fodder and grass (6:5), and a little salt for the tasteless food Eliphaz feeds him (6:6). But the God who could supply all this—and does, to the wild ass and the ox (6:5)—does not do so for Job, does not do so for man, but tests him, and makes much of him—as if he were very much more than an animal. Who would want this? But could God's love for a human being be anything like His love for a sparrow, or the stolid, cud-chewing cow, happy with the grass (6:5)? Would a lover wish for a pet? Could what Job says he wants be sufficient for a human being? And if it could not be sufficient for a man, could it be what love is for God?

A thousand sparrows could not make up the difference in the kind of love in which human beings may take part. That kind of love is somehow connected with justice; its precise nature philosophers and theologians will discuss until God makes it perfectly clear, but Job suffers this connection between love and justice in his flesh: Job is not yet

clear about this dilemma; he is suffering it. One part of
Job's plaint starts here: man is exalted (7:17); he can know
and participate in the eternal justice which is God. And Job
has; this has been his daily communion, as God knows.
That justice is God Himself, and to be able to participate in
it—at every moment—is God's loving gift. Justice itself—
that is God—cannot be brought into corruption by even
the greatest sin of a creature of dust, and that is the source
of Job's complaint—if I sin, what do I do to thee (7:20)?
Why cannot God's love "pardon my offense or take away
my guilt?" But then the other side of the problem shows
itself: what becomes of the gift of participation in God,
which gift makes the beloved worth more than a thousand
sparrows? The same thing which exalts man makes him
into God's target (7:12, 6:4); having such a nature introduces expectation, something one may fulfill or fail at. To
disconnect God's love from His justice would transform us
again into pets. God's love lifts us far above that animal
nature, the strictness of His concern takes His vision from
the very core of our being out to the swallowing of our spit:
become perfect, even as your heavenly Father is perfect.

That the Almighty himself should be concerned with
this dust, should watch it and sift it by His own hand—is
that not itself an honor far above any creature's deserving?
An honor and a privilege, but also a terror beyond our
bearing, as Job himself, here, bears out? Then let us not
think of it as an honor, for it is a terror beyond even Job's
bearing, and there is none like him on the earth. To think
of it as an honor to be sifted by the hand of God is to lead
oneself into temptation; for Job—who is righteous—here
testifies only to the terror:

> For the arrows of the almighty are in me,
> my soul drinks their poison,
> the terrors of God arrayed against me. (6:4)

Before God, who can stand? Who can even desire to stand in that gaze?

But who could desire not to, ever?

Fear of the Lord, for Job, is not the mere *Realpolitikal* fear of the weak for the omnipotent, but the moral terror of absolute answerability—even for the swallowing of one's spit. This answerability is the effect of God's love, his perfect attention. For a spiritual being, every act is a token of gratitude and praise—or not. Everything is accepted as a gift, because that is what the created order is—or not. Each moment. Which of us has paid sufficient attention? Whoever is not a perfectly religious poet in every moment of his life is subject to the terrorism of God, for everything at every moment is an inscape to the graciousness of the divine—or else is a booby trap to remind us that it is an inscape to the grace of the divine. It is difficult to be a poet at all times. It is more difficult to be so on Job's ash-heap at death's door, but we note that all his speeches are in verse.

Anselm saw the same stringency of love and justice when he posed this problem:

> If you should find yourself in the sight of God, and one said to you: "Look thither;" and God, on the other hand, should say: "It is not my will that you should look;" ask your own heart what there is in all existing things which would make it right for you to give that *look* contrary to the will of God . . . ; whether you can do it even for your own salvation . . . [or] if it were necessary that the whole universe, except God Himself, should perish and fall

back into nothingness, [if you did not] do so small a thing against the will of God?

...

What if there were more worlds as full of beings as this?[1]

For nothing in the world—not the whole world, or even a universe of worlds—can it be right to turn and even *look* elsewhere: will you not look away even long enough for me to swallow my spit?

We might be able to think of the difficulty in these terms: Job's earlier happiness and praise was at the immanence of God. God was present to Job in and through all of creation—the world bloomed, his animals multiplied; his visible hopes and joys made love's justice seem easy, and his virtues, too, were a conscious participation in the being of God. What makes praise—love's justice—seem impossible now is that all of this man's—Job's—hope stands outside of the world—in the words of the Holy One, which he has not denied. The mortal halo has disappeared and the only virtue to be practiced on the ash-heap is a negative one: not to curse God. But does not hope have to work *in* the world? Upon the world? With the world? None of that is available to Job. Precisely the complete transcendence of his hope now is what feels like the poison of God's arrows—the transcendent is too far away for a *body* to get to. He can't connect. Just here Job has no recourse—the recourse of the stone is lacking to him, for he feels pain; and the recourse of the animal has not been given, for he has neither stall nor grass, and besides, he knows (as the animal

---

[1] St Anselm, *Cur Deus Homo?* translation by Sidney Norton Deane in *Proslogium; Monologium; An appendix in behalf of the fool by Gaunilon; and Cur Deus Homo*, chapter 21.

does not) that God is watching him bear it, even to the swallowing of his spit. He can't give up bearing it; only God can release him. *In extremis*, Job confesses that hope in this transcendent lover tastes like poison. But Job does swallow it; he keeps his hope. His hope is that he be released from this unbearable position. *In extremis*, praise comes forth as lamentation and a request that he be done quickly. Is there anyone like Job upon the earth?

JOB 8

Bildad the Shuhite

BILDAD IS ANGRY. Not exactly at Job, yet, but at Job's teaching that God's justice is not perfectly retributive. Where Eliphaz's first speech implied that Job may have some fault, Bildad openly accuses Job's children:

> Does God pervert justice?
> Or does the Almighty distort the right?
> Your children sinned against Him
> and He delivered them unto their transgression.
> (8:3–4)

He is not responding to what Job has said; in fact, he thinks Job's speech is just a big wind, one that avoids the point at issue: God is just; the world is His; therefore the evil that happens to a person is a result of being delivered into the power of the transgression he has enjoyed. This argument is deductive; he does not hear the counterpoint about God's love which Job had been sounding out; nor does he consider that suffering might be to exhibit virtue—as God is sure Job will. Nor, it goes without saying, could it ever be salvific, as the exhibition of Job's virtue might be for his wife, or for one or another of the sons of heaven. The practical conclusion is straightforward:

> If you are pure and upright
> surely He will rouse Himself for you. (8:6)

And on the other side, to trust other than in God and His justice is to hang on gossamer, or lean on the house of the spider (8:13–15). Bildad's irony approaches sarcasm in his mockery of such persons:

> While yet in flower and not cut down
> they wither before any other plant...
> Behold, this is the joy of his way
> and out of this dust others sprout up. (8:12–19)

Bildad is right about the ways of sin: to live in them is to wither one's own being; even vegetables have more life and sense. Bildad does not, however, go quite so far as to accuse Job himself of taking a place among these happy dust-sprouts—he probably still has some faith in Job's reputation. Instead, he closes by encouraging Job that God will yet fill his mouth with laughter. He believes Job is blameless; and now, the problem of his (sinful) children being resolved, he need merely remind God of his blamelessness in order to recover his rights. And so at the close Bildad sounds quite different; as if he considers that God, in hurling his thunderbolts at the obviously sinful children of Job, caused some minor collateral damage among Job's sheep and on Job himself; but when Job reminds God of his justice all things will be well—in fact, better: "Your former state will be of little moment" (8:7).

Like Eliphaz, who, in saying that God would keep Job hidden "from the roving tongue" and from "fear of the demon when he comes" (5:21), seemed to be near the mark about the real story of Job, which, in part (i.e., the part of the demons), his friends are enacting, Bildad now suggests something we have heard before too. He proves the fairy tale was never a separate story. For, the roving son of heaven had also said that the deaths of one's children could not be a real test of one's love for God, that since it doesn't strike his own flesh it isn't serious. Bildad here suggests Job will yet flourish even more (8:7) and God will yet fill his mouth with laughter and his lips with shouts of joy (8:21). He thereby agrees with the roving tongue's earlier thesis that the death of all the children whom he loves is something the old patriarch will be able to get over easily enough. If he gets up early (8:6) and prays honestly, he will get God's reward and things will be perfectly well with him. They imagine fatherhood to be about the welfare of the father. Bildad imagines fatherhood as Eliphaz had imagined justice—an accident of being, not a way of being.

Two friends in a row have now echoed things that only God and the adversary know about, and if they are not—as we discover they are not—speaking God's side, there must be someone else whose tongue has gotten into their mouths. The recommendation of Job's easy recovery from the loss of his beloved children, the suggestion that they must have sinned and deserved their deaths added into the bargain, brings into human terms the dilemma of love and justice which underlay Job's answer to Eliphaz. Here we see that Bildad apparently thinks love is having what you want, that what a patriarch wants is goods and children, but that these are all replaceable tokens, like pets, not individuals. But if we are offended at Bildad's suggestion about a father's love, should we not be more offended to think of God's love as in any way similar?

A further problem in Bildad's speech is his suggestion that while Job's children unquestionably deserved what they got—that they got God's lightning proves they deserved it—the just Job looks to have been accidentally singed. If

Job goes to God early and wakes Him, He will restore Job's domain (8:5–6). But if there are these minor problems with lightning control, what of Bildad's mathematically exacting lesson from the wisdom of our fathers (8:8)? Is it not itself a house of gossamer and spider thread? For if God's justice is occasionally inexact—as in its scorching of Job while (justly) burning his children—then there is no such thing as exact justice; it is a delusion and trick of the light. And then there is the issue upon which any court case turns, the *quaestio facti*—the question of fact—did Job's children sin? And if they did, and so greatly as to be driven to dust, *can* Job's mouth be filled with laughter ever again? Should we expect that he can he know happiness, knowing that? We have palpated the self-involved tumor of which this thought is a disincarnate symptom in chapter two. Bildad's repetition of it does not bode well for his judgment; he seems to have forgotten the meaning of Job's early morning sacrifices; this day he has forgotten all ten of the sacrifices Job never failed to remember on any previous day. Bildad's speech fails, then, both on the side of justice and on the side of love. For him we must feel pity, for he does not know what he is talking about. His speech fails in justice, for it judges without knowing the facts; and it fails in love, for it forgets that love desires the good for the beloved even if the beloved fails and falls into sin. Bildad, however, presumes that the beloved sinners can be written off and forgotten. He is like a utilitarian speaking of justice in an economy, "a compensation of quantity," as Aquinas puts it.[1] As if love is for rewards; as Lear speaks of love... to Cordelia.

---

[1] Aquinas, *Literal Exposition*, 159.

On *Job*

The world is the Lord's, and Bildad himself says so, but he does not know *how* it is the Lord's, or how completely and exactly even the dust of it is sifted.

JOB 9–10
Job's Reply

THERE IS A TRUE SENTENCE in Bildad, and this sentence Job hears: That God is indeed just. "I know well that it is so" (9:2), he says. In fact, he knows it more deeply than Bildad, for he sees that what follows from this is not the world Bildad presumes—of light for the children of light and darkness for the others—but a world far more problematic, for "how can a man be just before God?" (9:2) If *God* is indeed just, then let us consider further. Let us consider, along with his justice, his wisdom and power, and these three inseparable. If this God—who made the stars and can turn the earth over on its axis, who treads on the back of the sea-monster and yet passes by Job's face without a whisper of wind (9:5–11)—if this being is "indeed just," then does the word even have an analogy for us? Can what we—or Bildad—call justice even be counted as one part of a thousand in comparison (9:3)? What common denominator can there be between this "indeed just" of the creator and creatural dust? Is not even the rhyme scheme of human language a thoroughly inaccurate and incapable abomination? Is it even, yet, language? Have we learned to speak?

There is infinitely good reason, then, for Job to say:

> Though I am innocent, I cannot answer Him.
> I would defend myself by begging for mercy.

On *Job*

If I summoned and He answered
I could not believe He heard me. (9:15-16)

For what of the divine could my justice touch? And what
could my words mean to the being who *is* justice? And the
power of creation. And wisdom itself. Though I were
indeed innocent, would not my own speaking in the face of
this infinite difference be a confession of criminal mispri-
sion? A foolishness not to be ventured. Though I were
blameless, would not such speech be proof that I am perverse? For what I would be attempting would be to make
myself an understandable and justified fraction of God:
sharing in the very being of justice. It would be to say that
eternal justice can be played out, without loss, by a creature,
in time. Bildad and Eliphaz both believe in exactly this—
justice visible: to sinners the appropriate fraction of suffering, to the good a rational number of goodies. To claim justice in the face of God, who is indeed just, is to presume
there is a bar before which we both can be summoned and
judged. And to request this is to request that God put off
His Godness—in order to be serious with us. And is this
not to presume that God is, possibly, not indeed just? —for
there is, now, a bar before him; a bar at which measure can
be made, analogy drawn. All these consequences Job sees,
but Bildad *cannot* see it, so Job, in disgust, answers him:

I am innocent;
I care not for myself;
I loathe my life.
It is all one. (9:21-22)

Bildad spoke of justice as a rational fraction. Job understands that, since *God—He who is*—is indeed just, we are
all irrational numbers. His conclusion in the lines above is,

78

therefore, exactly correct. For if we are all irrational subtrahends of the infinite circle, our terms forever incapable of adding up correctly, then even perfect innocence (as we figure it) should, knowing this, not care what it adds up to, and in fact loathe the attempted addition, recognize it as an infringement upon holiness, an impertinence to the giver of being, and *prefer* to be zero, which is at least in the right number system, for in ours it is all one—innocence and guilt, blamelessness and evil—none of us have learned how to count.

> Teach us to care and not to care.
> Teach us to sit still.[1]

Given this, Job suggests an entirely different solution, one which Bildad's mathematics avoids only by the blasphemy of bringing God before the same bar as man. Knowing "thou wilt not hold me innocent," knowing "I shall be condemned, why then do I labor in vain?" (9:28–29), knowing that though he be innocent as a human being, before God there is no way to dress him in the clothes of the acquitted (9:29–31)—and certainly there is no requirement to dress him in the glad rags of reward, for what is the most perfect human justice save the bare accomplishment of an absolute duty?—knowing all this, Job sees the solution: If God is indeed just, there is no bar before which Job, or any man, can plead. Therefore Job loathes his life (10:1). And he loathes it *because* justice is all he has sought and now it has come home to him that there is no way for this irrational fraction to find his solution.

"Therefore, I will complain" (10:1). Why do you make

---

[1] T. S. Eliot, "Ash Wednesday," part VI, lines 26–27.

me like this? Does it seem good to you to despise, to oppress the work of your hands? What, in fact, could be more oppressing? If God is trying to make clay pots and charge them with divine commands, then should he not at least look at us with eyes of flesh when He judges? What is the point of this game of making men out of dirt and then expecting the divinity of justice to appear in them and then smash them when, inevitably, it does not? This economy is unbearably stupid. It is unbearable. It is stupid. It is not an economy. Counting, in the presence of the infinite: who would do that? Lose, or lose:

> If I sin, Thou dost mark me... ,
> if I am righteous, I cannot lift my head. (10:14–15)

Why doesn't He just let us be, for life is short and the land of darkness is deep indeed? But my complaint is not the proper tone for prayer.

> What shall I say, my God, my justice, my holy delight? Or what does anyone say when he speaks of You? Yet woe to those who say nothing, for even the mouths of those who say much are as the dumb.[2]

---

[2] *Conf.* 1.4.4.

JOB 11

Zophar the Naamathite

ZOPHAR *IS* ANGRY, so much so and in such a way that we have to reconsider Job's previous speech. He accuses Job of senseless babbling and worse; he accuses him of saying to God, "my teaching is pure and I am clean in your sight" (11:4). Against this, Zophar hopes for God to declare Job's sins to him, since he is apparently so forgetful of them. He proclaims Job a fool, his complaint as unlikely as a tame ass being born of a wild one (11:12). No doubt Zophar means this figure also to apply literally to Job—he is really a wild ass who has perhaps fooled others into thinking he is a tame one, but God knows better and is in the process of breaking him into a more useful beast—one having under-standing. Having castigated him, Zophar catechizes in the usual manner: remove the iniquity from your conduct and injustice from your tent, then you may stand firm and unafraid with nothing to disturb you (11:13–19).

But Job, we know, has not been unfaithful to the Lord, nor is his ignorance of guilt due to lack of self-examination. It was, in fact, his wont to offer sacrifice every morning for all his children for the sake of things which he could neither see nor have any reason even to impute—his sacrifices were offered on behalf of innocence in case there was some unno-ticed flaw. Nor has Job claimed to be blameless *tout court.* In the multitude of words Zophar has just listened to, he apparently did not hear that Job spoke conditionally—"though I am innocent my own mouth would condemn me" (9:20)—or if not conditionally, he has drawn a far from positive conclusion—"I am blameless; I regard not myself; I loathe my life" (9:21). He is not full of himself; he does not make claims to stand up before God. Indeed, Job has wondered deeply where his own flaw is, and not having seen one he has come to a far more sublime question: "How can a man be justified before God" (9:2)? To consider the powerful beauty, greatness, and holiness of God is to know that even innocence is made of clay, that even what is cleansed thoroughly is unable by its own power to wear the garment which God might give to the acquitted. Even the good are unable to bear such scrutiny, and from this view "it is all one. Both the innocent and the wicked are destroyed" (9:22). To truly consider God's holiness would make us evaporate like a drop of water fallen on a dry bone in the desert.

Zophar's speech misses Job entirely, so his anger then—sparked by Job's speech—must not be about what he claims it is about. There must be something in the speech that Zophar considers as blasphemous as what he (falsely) accuses Job of—or perhaps just something more troubling, something he does not wish to face. Zophar's anger must be at the fact that Job has come to the point of saying that even righteousness is unworthy of God's notice. And there is only one reason to be so angry at this: Zophar must wish to have something of his own to hang on to before God. He must wish to have something that is of note to bring before the face of God—righteousness—on which he may "stand firm and unafraid" (11:15). Zophar must consider it possible for a life to be made bright by its own goodness, and secure before God in its innocence. Under such a circumstance "many shall entreat your favor" (11:19), for from the rock of one's own innocence much favor may be granted without loss of security. He is angry at the thought that his own goodness—his own dedication to the law— could be accounted nothing; that Job seems to see that it *is* nothing: a whole life of justice is as a grain of sand before the wind. The theodicide wishes for his own justice, a human justice, to count; as if a clay pot could hold the fathomless sea, or a grain of sand the real glory of God.

Zophar is not a complete idiot, he merely fails to see what is in his power and what is not. He seems to think that there can be a limit to gratitude, a mathematical cusp at which human goodness or human justice contributes something positive to the divine economy, perhaps a point on the curve where we earn our keep and God breaks even on his creation. Zophar does have part of the story right. We should still act upon Zophar's catechism and remove iniquity from our conduct, injustice from our tent, but even then what are we but profitless servants? Or what have we done besides our duty and what is, at a minimum, required? And what is it for such a one to *expect happiness*? To claim it as an effect owed to goodness? And what threat hangs over the one who, being happy, considers that his righteousness deserves it? Guarantees it? Makes it safe? Can nothingness, granted freedom and being, hold a claim against He Who Is, against Being and Love? What does it mean to *want* to? Is not Zophar's anger horribly frightening? It fills me with dread and terror. What Zophar says of the impious seems to be coming back at him; as another translation has it, "their hope is the abomination of the soul" (11:20).[1]

---

[1] Aquinas quotes the Vulgate; *Literal Exposition*, 199, 201.

On *Job*

May a sinner pray for a righteous man? But I already have too much to beg for myself. And if Zophar has *misunderstood*, he has not, knowing the truth of some matters, *disobeyed*.

JOB 12-14

Job's Reply to Zophar

THAT JOB FEELS MOCKED by his friends is clearer from his opening sarcasm—"no doubt you are noble / and with you wisdom will die" (12:2)—than from the lines following (12:4), which seem more a complaint. Not only has Zophar said nothing new, but his "wise speech" expresses the generally hidden and thoughtless contempt that the comfortable have for those in calamity—a contempt which we sometimes see more faithfully expressed in a kind of uncharitable pity. When a person is rich and has power—"carries his god in his fist" (12:6)—he may sometimes, out of the overflow of his confidence and in the optimism to which power raises him, deign to bestow good upon the downtrodden. Nietzsche, for example, praises this kind of charity. It is the earthly city's version of humility. But such a man's act, like Zophar's speech, is beneath the wisdom of the beasts and birds. All the animals of earth know that they are in God's hand (12:7–8); none is so foolish as to think that God is in theirs, that wisdom or good is theirs to bestow. The ear that tests Zophar's words tastes blasphemy (12:11): "*With God* there is wisdom and right" (12:13), but Zophar has them not. His tone of supposed understanding and explanation treads upon ground that is not his. All earth's counselors, all her judges and kings, her priests, her elders, her confident princes (12:17–21), have a wisdom that is darkness by comparison to God's, and their own power is as that of a drunk (12:25). This darkness we can confer of our own power. But from the wisdom of God comes a light which reveals that all human wisdom is indeed darkness (12:22); His lightning deprives the confident of speech, as we saw with Job earlier, and reveals as rags the fine clothes of kings and of counselors.

Zophar, without knowing, has put himself among these "wise" men, but it is clear to Job that no man can answer his question. "I would speak with Shaddai" (13:3); silence on the part of the friends would be wisdom. For what in fact are they trying to do? Is it within the power of man, or of man's mind, to defend God? To come into court as a witness in His defense—perhaps even a character witness? But they defend Him by lying about Job; is this the way to dare do God a favor—by lying about Him? And if you do not have the wisdom of God will not your defense in any case be a lie? And necessarily so? Is this a wise move—to attempt to give evidence in this trial? So much for theodicy. What if God should probe you (13:9) to see whether the witness has the character capable even of defending himself? Does not the fear of the Lord overwhelm you (13:11)? Can ashes and clay do such service? We should beware that even our desire to *stand* on the side of the all-good might be found corrupt. And so, to *defend* it...? Should we then, with regard to God, always wish to be in the wrong?

Zophar clearly wishes to be in the right. Not necessarily against God, but clearly against Job; no doubt there are others on his list as well. He thinks himself on God's side. Should we then always wish to be in the wrong before every other person? Job knows that God "will openly rebuke you if even in secret you show partiality" (13:16), which means he must himself have been careful of his conscience with everyone he met. Job lets Zophar know that he (Zophar) is in the wrong against him, and that he ought to fear that he might, by speaking so against him, also be in the wrong against God. So then, in acknowledging that we are in the wrong before God do we thereby admit being incapable of judging whether anyone else is so? When we imagined Job helping the injured in his early life, we imagined him saying, "does not your integrity bear you up?" We did not imagine him judging the injured to be evil, or even morally questionable. Job's *question* to such a one was medicine, for it was an assumption of the good—even if it led to an examination of conscience and repentance on the part of the one realizing he is not so. The just man dares not judge the suffering, for to judge presumes the wisdom of God: a thing the just man would never claim. On the other hand, Zophar's *explanation* of Job's suffering—that it is due to his sin—leads Job to call Zophar a quack healer, and Job warns him lest he step over the human line and presume a righteousness and capacity which in fact are not his before God. He is *declarative* about Zophar's error regarding himself; he is *interrogative* about the possible error of Zophar before God: "Will it be well with you when he probes you?" (13:9). In raising the question of justice to another human being we are invoking this higher power; we should be, then, in terror of error ourselves. For suppose he who is justice comes. Another teacher will say, "let him who is without sin cast the first stone." This is good advice, for if we take it, we will never err on the side of judgment, and who would wish to enter into judgment? Doing so is calling upon divine justice, which shows no partiality, and needs not our defense. Let us not make any assumptions about our neighbor's evil, lest we ourselves be probed to our depths. Job does not presume. Zophar does.

Job drops the question of Zophar and addresses God again. He knowingly—unlike (I assume) Zophar—takes his own flesh in his teeth. He girds himself to face the probing of God—though not, be it noted, through accusation of another; rather, by presenting himself: he feels he has nothing to lose. Perhaps, in fact, his suffering is God's probing, and the comforting of his friends is its continuance. Satan, at any rate, is proving something. But the world and everything in it are in God's hand, and the probing and the eye do not pause for rest. That was Job's earlier complaint (7:18–20; 10:20); we should suspect that even now Job is inspecting his words, for they are scrutinized by a far higher power—whether they go as far as his lips or no. We have already noticed that Job, even in his anger, does not presume that Zophar has done injustice before God; he only points out that his speech is unwise and mistaken about himself (Job). In fact, the friends' judgement of Job implicates them in speaking falsely for God (13:7); they "speak deceitfully" that suffering is always punishment and judge that saying so defends divine justice. But the Just One needs no defense, and what must a man be thinking of himself to think he can give one? Certainly, then, He will not abide a lying defense. Perhaps we should never ask if we are being tested, for to do so is to confess forgetfulness, and this forgetfulness is sin. The test is upon us even now; for God is ever present. Perhaps happiness itself is a test which it is possible to fail. Job seems to have understood this, and he failed not in his happiness. Now the other side of the test is upon him: suffering. And it is terminal. But here, what is there for a man to hang on to? Not even hope. So it seems.

Job remembers everything: "I will defend my conduct to his face; though he slay me, I will not quaver" (13:15). He knows such a claim is foolishness added to impiety if one has any doubts. Speaking as a man before men, he has none. "I know I will be acquitted" (13:18). Then he asks God to tell him his sins, to count them up, not to write him down as mere inheritor of his youthful iniquity, but to declare how the responsible man has failed and become worthy of treatment as an enemy of God. Like many of the psalms, this is not a prayer I wish to repeat on my own behalf. Only the just man can be driven into this terrible dilemma between the impossibility of seeing justice at work in the world and the self-immolation of abandoning justice as a mirage. Only a man between these two horns can lament as Job does. Before Job I myself would prefer to be silent, and, if forced to speak, beg his indulgence that I do not suffer as he does. Perhaps this lets us see how we must look upon the suffering of others: "May your servant be allowed to bring you a glass of water?" Might it not be the case that the happy and untested (such as Zophar and I) have duties in the face of suffering that are as deep as the suffering? Might it not be the case that community with the suffering and those being tested is not a supererogatory virtue, but always and merely our duty—and the lightest duty a human being may ever be given? O God, come to my assistance; O Lord, make haste to help me.

Job's complaint to God takes that same tone before God as I would before Job:

> Man born of woman,
> short-lived, sated with strife;
> like a flower he comes forth and withers,

like a shadow he flits, never staying.
He wastes away like a rotten thing,
like a garment eaten by moths.
And on such would you turn your gaze
and bring him into judgment before you?
(13:28–14:3)

This complaint, we should note, does not concern injustice. Though Job earlier (13:18) says he will be acquitted, *he is not*, in here addressing God, *accusing Him of injustice*. His complaint is that life is short and miserable, and once it is over what is there? We are less than the vegetables,

for a tree though cut down has hope...
though its stump die in the dust
at the scent of water it will bud.
But a man dies and where is he?
(14:7–10)

Job's complaint to God is not about justice, but about happiness. But that he complains to God about this matter is our reminder of the earlier Job: he will take his happiness only from the hand of God. He will not carve for himself (like that happy and blessed man who has his god in his fist). He wishes for happiness as the dead stump wishes for the scent of water, but he will not *take it* for himself. He wishes to be hidden in Sheol until God's anger passes—if it would pass and he could be happy. He is willing to wait in the land of the dead if God will give him, someday, time and remembrance.

But mountains topple and crumble,
the rock is moved from its place,

the waters wear away stones
and floods wash out the soil

—and so God destroys Job's hope (14:18–19). Whole life-
times, whole generations and peoples fail to find water. His
own flesh pains him, and his soul mourns itself (14:22).

It is curious that among the things Job would count as
happiness when he imagines God turning toward him
again, ages hence, is this: "that my guilt would be sealed in
a bundle and you would coat over my iniquity" (14:17). It is
hard not to see here that Job's long, broken request is a hope
whose outrageousness he cannot yet fully shape; that from
death, long after the tumbling of the mountains and the
washing of the shore back into the sea, he should be raised
up to a life in God's eye, with his sins sealed in the bag of the
old earth—the mountains have fallen on it, and it is buried
in the sea. It is as if Job knows that the end of life on earth
will come when the sun, grown to a red giant in its long
death throes, melts the very earth into its core as it expands
beyond our present orbit and then collapses into a cold dark
star, and then goes out. We should not think it strange,
however, that the just man's waking visions are true, or his
dreams prophetic. Rather we should expect that only such
as these can see. The longer I live the more I think that in
this prayer—that my guilt be sealed in a bundle and coated
over, and after the wrath is past He would remember me—
is hidden the only prayer a serious man would ever make:
for the forgiveness of sins, and the resurrection of the body.
But perhaps I do not yet know what seriousness is. In all
events, this is a prayer I can share in; in fact, I find it to be
perfect; were it to be answered there would be nothing I
should want. I am happy within this prayer; without it my
soul mourns itself and my flesh pains me.

JOB 15

Eliphaz's Second Speech

HAVING HEARD JOB suggest that the defense of God given by his comforters might well be at the expense of truth (13:7–12) and is, in any case, daring, since it invites the probing of God, Eliphaz is no longer polite. He calls Job a wind-bag and worse, one whose speech does away with fear of the Lord and lessens devotion to God. But this makes it perfectly clear that Job and his comforters are having one of those discussions in which neither hears the other; at least, all of his friends have misheard Job. And perhaps the point of the book is to show us this: the idea that suffering is punishment for the sins of the sufferer is so ingrained that a speech which brings it into question is heard as blasphemy and a condemnation from one's own mouth and lips (15:6). But Job has done or said nothing to do away with fear of the Lord; in fact, nothing is more obvious than that he practices it with each word. He has called up for question the materialist interpretation of the literal truth of an ancient axiom: evil to the evil, good to the good; and his friends hear blasphemy and self-promotion. But we have seen how, hidden in their accusation, is self-forgetfulness— if not blasphemy. For all of them, Eliphaz most obviously, have forgotten the question whether anyone can be just before God. They have forgotten to consider whether any-one can stand before the All Holy. Perhaps the literal and materialist truth they are at pains to defend is itself a mishearing of the statement that God is justice. How better to show this than through this constant mishearing of Job?

All Job's comforters, like Eliphaz, respond with an anger that both sounds like and includes self-defense:

> Are you the first-born of mankind?
> Were you brought forth before the hills?
> Are you privy to the counsels of God,
> and limit wisdom to yourself?
> What do you know that we do not know,
> or what intelligence have you that we lack?
> We have gray hairs and age among us. (15:7–10)

But Eliphaz's speech *does* exactly that of which he *accuses* Job: it limits intelligence to the friends—as Job had suggested: "No doubt you are the intelligent folk and with you wisdom shall die" (12:2). Eliphaz presumes upon the counsel of God to know how He judges and why He does what He does. In doing so such a one presumes intimacy with the justice which is God. (But before Him who can stand?) This time, no perturbation of a dream gives Eliphaz pause as it did earlier (ch. 4). He returns directly to his argument from the ancient generic truth to Job's specific case: "If in his holy ones He places no confidence . . . how much less so . . . in man?" (15:15–16). But again, if Eliphaz's argument is true, he should be silent—for what is one such as he doing by daring to defend the Most High? If in His holy ones He places no confidence, how much less so in Eliphaz... The *fact of* his speaking belies *what* his speech says. The dream which disturbed his first speech was the truest thing about him. What is it if a man is only true in his dreams?

Perhaps Eliphaz's problem (and that of all the other friends as well) is the literalism of his understanding of God's wisdom. He takes it, for example, that the rest of his speech—15:20–35—is empirically "showable":

> I will show you, hear me;
> what I have seen I will tell;
> what wise men relate
> and have not contradicted.
> (15:17–18)

And what he tells of is the life of the wicked, but he expects it to be a visible truth—that

> the wicked man writhes in pain all his days...
> and in prosperity, the spoiler comes upon him.
> (15:20–21)

It is clear that this view was popular in the ancient Near East; it was accounted wisdom in ancient Israel and surrounding lands, before a belief in resurrection rose among a group that became known as the Pharisees. Is ancient Judaism, then, despair? Does it hold as a fundamental truth that justice is empirically provable—that it plays out in happiness in the finite world, and life gives us our exact reward? Can the Jew be satisfied in time and space? Is Judaism stuck, exactly, in the finite? Can it be that while God is spirit, man takes no part in that life? It is true that much of the Old Testament holds that "piety is your assurance," but if, for all that, ancient Judaism is not despair, it is because it asks also, "can a man be just before God?" And this question implies the recognition that the human measurement of justice is a form of foolishness whenever it is not blasphemy; and such a recognition only spiritual beings can have.

Eliphaz's Second Speech

Job is canonical for the Jews, despite the fact that its hero is not a Jew, despite the fact that it is not a national saga, and despite the fact that it seems almost blasphemously to take God to task, precisely because it dares to seek a path between the wisdom of the legalistic philosophers, who consider piety assurance, and the transcendence of the all-holy God, which raises an entirely opposite question— whether it has entered the heart of man to imagine what justice, piety, or assurance is.[1] The poet of the book of Job sought rightly, and to seek rightly is the first gift of the spirit. In sifting us through this terrible dilemma the poet of the book of Job shows us, under the literalism of Eliphaz, a deeper understanding of happiness, as of justice— and their opposites: his language lets it appear that for the wicked, the spoiler is already upon him (15:21); that such a one already dwells in a ruined city and a desolate house (15:28)—one already crumbling and offering no shadow under the bright sun of God's eye. Since God is not with him, such hopes as he has are vain—it is as if the goods of the wicked are not really there at all, for it is vanity for a spirit to hope in something other than spirit, and such hopes achieved are themselves a condemnation. *And such a one is living in it. And happy.* He dwells in houses that are deserted and in cities that are abandoned (15:28). He dwells there, but there is no he there, and there is no dwelling. He does not know the place where he is, and he does not see it.

---

[1] These two issues (the assurance of piety, and the impossibility of human imagination grasping it) are the reason for Fr. Gutierrez's remark that any talk about God has to include two languages—the language of mysticism (which has its eye on the transcendence of God) and the language of prophecy (which has its eye on the demand for justice which God's love requires). Cf. Gutierrez, *On Job*, 95.

On *Job*

The poet's imagery here strikes me as a sort of film negative, a reversal of another famous poet's image—perhaps they were even living at the same time. Homer tells us of Cassandra, who on a quiet afternoon walks on the still-standing walls of Troy and suddenly is screaming of fire and destruction, madly seeing it, feeling it, experiencing the crumbling of the towers, the terror in her flesh, the burning in her feet though the Greeks are not yet even encamped around her happy city. So the poet of *Job* envisions the wicked: they seem to be living in a well-built and finely appointed mansion, but already it is empty, broken down and abandoned. From the God's-eye point of view the only mortar for a city's stones is justice, and a house or city not built this way has no jointure, though like the walls of siegeless Troy they look for all the world as though they can be calmly tread upon. It is not that the walls of the wicked will fall; they already have "no shadow to lengthen over the ground" (15:29).

This horror seems to be how Job understands wickedness, at any rate. One who makes sacrifice for the accidental forgetfulness of his children must see clearly the emptiness and vanity, sterility and failure of a life attempting to hide from the light of God's eye. Job's complaint about God's constant watchfulness has verified that such is his understanding of things. The wicked, who live on the fat of the land, hide under a mask of folly (15:27): they think that happiness is pleasure, not knowledge of God and grateful obedience. With Eliphaz Job would say, "they give birth to failure" (15:36), though it may not be visible. Or, I should say, it is certainly not visible to Eliphaz; his vision has the flatness of empirical science. The only way his vision will be changed is if God should appear in the world, for that is all he can see: the world. But even if God would appear in the world, the question about Eliphaz would be, could he see the God in the world?

> Let him not trust in emptiness, deceiving himself;
> for emptiness will be his recompense.
> It will be paid in full ahead of time. (15:31–32)

To be mistaken about happiness is already to have nothing—even when having everything. The man who is speaking is already there: *de te fabula narratur.*[2]

---

[2] The Latin phrase, "the story is told about you," is from a poem by Horace, but I always think of it in connection with Samuel's story of the rich man taking the poor man's lamb; after hearing the story David condemns that man, and Samuel says, "you are the man" (2 Sam 12:1–7).

JOB 16–17

Job's Response

IN THE PREFACE of his "Answer to Job," Carl Jung proposes to "give expression to the shattering emotion which the unvarnished spectacle of divine savagery and ruthlessness produces in us,"[1] but Job's response to Eliphaz in this continuing interchange of speeches gives more expression to misery compounded with disgust at the constant misunderstanding of his "miserable comforters" (16:2) than to divine savagery. Job gives notice that he could be as windy, provoking, and haranguing as his friends—were he in their position—or he could give them solace by his words; but as things are with him, whether he speaks or no his misery is unchanged and God has worn him out: his company is desolate and desolating. Though he says, "God has given me up to the ungodly" (16:11), Job's complaint sounds much more like a complaint against humanity around him than against the God who fails to appear at his request. The complaint is most particularly against the visiting friends and the painfulness of human companionship, rather than against God's savagery and ruthlessness. And perhaps this is something that the most terrible suffering might drive someone to—to despair of man, to disgust with human uselessness in the face of uttermost need and exhaustion of

<hr />

[1] Jung, "Answer to Job," 366.

spirit. For what indeed can we contribute in such a situation? After all the more natural evil (lightnings, hurricanes),

> he sets me up as his target,
> and his archers surround me. (16:13)

> My friends scorn me;
> my eye pours out tears to God. (16:20)

> My spirit is broken and my days are extinct...
> Surely there are mockers about me,
> and my eye dwells upon their provocation.
> (17:1–2)

And there is no answer, no light from heaven, no light from Weimar beyond the hill.

For who really can be one with us in our suffering? Who, even with his weeping, can assuage what gives every indication of being our terminal pain? ("The grave is ready for me . . . who is there that will give surety for me?" [17:1–3].) And those who come, what can that mean except that one's suffering has become a byword? For being unable to share what is most terrible of suffering, they can come only to hear the story, or to watch. For the man whose "days are past," whose "plans are broken off" (17:11)—what can the ordinary human being with a past that is still meaningful, with a future still holding hope, have to do? "Shall we go down together to the gates of Sheol? Shall we descend together to the dust?" (17:18). But only one will go, and the other will remain. How can the visitors even connect, except by sight? If we speak of the past we are picking at his scabs: the children, the flocks, the happy feasts. If we speak of the future he is not there. How can a heart still distended between past and future share in the utter loss and devastation of a heart cut off from them both in the house at the door of Sheol? Perhaps their silence was indeed their friendship. The friends' speech aligns them with the satan: the traducer who "speaks openly against me; I am the prey his wrath assails" (16:8–9).

Yet Job seems to expect that he should be able to speak with his friends, that they should be able to comfort him; he thinks that he could do so to them (16:5). But they are not in communion and he calls them windy, desolating mockers; he compares them to flatterers (17:5) and hypocrites (17:8). Clearly they are saying what they think, so what Job must mean by all these words about words is that the friends' words have no connection to reality—as those of flatterers and hypocrites do not. But Job's cry is his lifeblood, and his blood is a cry (16:18). The word and the flesh are one in him. And it seems that underlying Job's complaint is the realization that only when word and flesh are one, or only in a shared liturgical act before a witness on high, can there be any true communication between human beings, any words that are not wind and hypocrisy or mockery and provocation. But how often have any of us spoken under such complete awareness? We have been a wind, blowing and then ceasing. Only if there is a witness in heaven, a comforter and paraclete on high (16:19–21), can a man in Job's situation have any hope or even any conversation, for a man without past or future cannot in other men find anything but salt for his wounds, and darkness in their wisdom, and air in their talk. That is what Job finds, and he cries out for heaven's comforter (16:19). Only in an impossible future (suggested also in 14:16ff and 19:25ff)— or in an absolutely permanent present—can Job be joined to those yet living. Only by abandoning their own more comfortable present for the same impossible future—or the indivisible and eternal now—can any human comforter give any comfort at all. If *Job* is a comfort in sorrow, it is because Job himself greets us when we come to this door. And now we sit in the same doorway. But can we pray with *this* man, that God "may do justice for a mortal in his presence?" (16:21)—for that is what it is to be with Job.

JOB 18

Bildad's Second Speech

AFTER COMPLAINING YET AGAIN that Job is pretending that his comforters are as stupid as cattle, Bildad gives a single argument, turned through image after image, all of them ending in the person of Job and some quite literal aspect of his suffering. The speeches have become like Job's suffering itself—boring, redundant, pointless and impersonal. Like cancer, the metaphors metastasize from one locus to another, varying their shape, skipping illogically from one site to another, returning to an original focus to come to fulfillment, the pain shifting deliriously through the body and soul, always two steps behind the point of present attack. Job is one who "tears himself in his anger" (18:4); he lacks all light; though vigorous, his steps are hobbled. Terrors surround him; he is hunger-bitten, his skin consumed, his tent untrustworthy; he has no offspring, no survivor, no root, no branch. Like suffering itself the speeches must merely be borne, got through if possible; there is nothing to be learned, for the speech comes not from someone who listens and takes part, but from one who watches and supplies an equation. Even in its most colorful transformations and most sudden pains, there is a stupefaction in this process that transforms one into something just above a beast of burden—or just beneath one.

Bildad's argument begins with the presumption that God

and the law of retribution on earth are merely aspects of each other; for him they are the same: God is merely the impersonal law of vengeance perfected and naturalized, like what appears in Aeschylus's *Agamemnon,* when Clytemnestra claims no longer to be herself, but merely her daughter's fury (Erinys), called up by the king upon himself. Bildad's rhetorical question—"shall the earth be forsaken for you, or shall the rock be moved out of its place?" (18:4)—exhibits his thesis: the rock, the law of retribution, keeps the planet in its orbit—is the planet in its orbit; it will not be moved for the single individual. It does not move and it cannot be that an individual human being can stand against it. The thesis is illustrated by a whole list of particulars; each particular has happened to Job: read it and weep. That is to say, Job's sufferings are merely the incidents of the working of the law, the rock, which incidents prove that the law is still working and which working proves his guilt. He is exhibited as bearing the rock of retribution; therefore the law is being upheld and all is right with the world. Bildad draws the conclusion on which all Job's friends have exhibited their agreement:

> They of the west are appalled at his day,
> and horror seizes them of the east.
> Surely such are the dwellings of the ungodly,
> such is the place of him who knows not God.
> (18:20–21)

It is perhaps a point of no little interest to see that the materialism of Job's friends, their fixed idea that the justice of God plays itself out in the empirical world exactly, is the anchor which keeps them in the nominalist harbor where their words may blow as hard as they will, but never touch the reality of Job—which is to say their words are mere breath (*flatus vocis*), they never touch the just man, they never touch the suffering of the innocent. They can, then, hardly be binding up the wounds of their friend. For them, the suffering of the innocent cannot exist; thus it is fitting and right that their statements swing back upon them: surely such are the dwellings of the ungodly, such is the place of him who knows not God. But if there is a Word on high, as Job maintains, and if every other word ought to be spoken in this Word, then we can begin to imagine why Job finds the words of his comforters pestilential and tormenting.

JOB 19

Job's Response

AND JOB DOES FEEL the redundancy of these speeches, but he does not feel them as boredom or as "something to be gotten through." He takes them personally, as torture, as reproachful castigation multiplied by ten. Even if it were true that Job had sinned, that sin seems to have stayed within him; the comforters, at any rate, have not been able to name a single act in their repeated accusations, and he rightly asks, "are you not ashamed to abuse me so?" (19:3). If Job has sinned, his sin remains with him (19:4), but their errors of judgment and speech are as scourgings for a crime for which no evidence has been given—except the scourging... Let us not think on it. If we know of someone else's sin, correction is in order; perhaps, when repeated, public reproach; but under what circumstances could it be right to continuously castigate the *suffering* sinner (so he is called), particularly if one is unable to name a single wrong deed? Aquinas suggests that by this time "they ought to have ceased their affliction of the afflicted from embarrassment, at least, if not because of friendship."[1]

And then, we—the readers cast in the role of omniscience opened to us by the writer—know that Job is not a

[1] *Literal Exposition,* 264.

105

sinner; must not the accusers' speeches which afflict him with further pain then also afflict us, not with disgust or boredom, but with pity for the accusers' ignorance, or perhaps even dread that a true Omniscience might hear them? Might it not even stir up our anger against them? Job himself seems to warn his erstwhile friends in the broken verses at the end of this chapter (19:28–29): to accuse Job of holding the root of his own evil fate within him (in the hidden seed of his sin) is to dare the wrath and the sword of judgment. And he has an argument to prove it: *If* their idea of God is right and they make his humiliation an argument against him, then God is unjust (19:5–6). Their very theodicy is an accusation against God who has pulled up Job's hope like a tree (19:10), with no cause. Job speaks the theological conclusion (God is unjust) from the standpoint of the only person who has an insight into the empirical premise—the fact or lack of sin. Indeed, Job does not claim sinlessness here, only that God has afflicted him inequitably or unfairly (19:6). We know there is none like him on earth, but what sins must they think he is hiding to consider all that has happened "equitable"! Thus their impeachment strips Job of his glory (God has not) and takes the crown of high honor from him (19:9).

From Job's point of view, the friends' speeches are aggravating his injuries precisely because they require him to believe that God is evil; they enforce an empirical economy of debt and payment—and he knows his debt is not so high. At what point could someone like me say that? Have I arisen early every morning to offer the tenfold sacrifice of praise? Or rather skipped one and another of the ten, having the gift of a day in which to do so? I don't expect at any time to be able to make this argument, and Job, in any case, does not succumb to this argument; rather it raises him to that even more perfect song of verse 25. He condemns their argument, and goes his own way, clinging to God against the mechanical (and ever more maniacal) darkness of the comforters' argument.

To be merely bored, then, by the repetitious accusing speeches of the friends is to confess a lack of faith; it means one does not live under the same consciousness Job lives under—the consciousness of the presence of the Omniscient sifter of dust; it confesses to not paying attention to how one's words are heard in the air; it reveals the presumption that life is something other than the liturgical act of words being spoken within the Word. For someone who shares Job's consciousness of the presence of God, the interesting and the boring are not the categories with which one is allowed to judge the speeches or actions either of oneself or of others; if we do so, we are not sifting correctly. Most of us, being less perfect than Job, slip in and out of these categories—boring, interesting, morally corrupt, blasphemous. We sift for a while—mostly others and their words—then go have a beer. But our sifting has not been true.

Job realizes something else learned by those whose suffering is constant: he finds he is no longer at all interesting: he is walled up, stripped of glory and hope; brothers, kinsfolk, acquaintances, and intimate friends have been estranged and have abandoned him; he is repulsive to his wife, and servants do not even answer when he begs (19:8–19). Not only can nothing about him induce intimacy, or that happy knowledge of each other that underlies any community, but also the world is actively engaged in a siege against such intimacy with him (19:12): such is crippling illness—at least in the materialist's world. Suffering is like money in this way: those who have it get more. The more is contributed by those who have it not: Job's friends. Finally (19:22), Job hits upon a point at which he and we might expect his friends to share somewhat in his sorrows: if they really believed what they were saying, should it not be enough for them that the hand of God rests on his flesh, should they not be sufficiently satisfied with the fact that he is being well-sifted not to harp themselves on his evil and pride? Should they not be happy and satisfied to see him as he is—the evidence of the continuing justice of God?

Driven into such straits—not merely the utter vacuity of the world, but its thorough antagonism, not just the absence of God, but (according to all the world) His enmity—what is it that holds the just man up? Given no ground, where does he even sit to beweep his fate? Job is driven there, and then he reveals the deepest secret of the just man, for the root of the matter *is* found in him, but the root in Job is not sin. Pushed outside of the world Job sets up his monument in it, chiseled in stone and inlaid with leading and precious stones: the witness of time to the eternal within it. Let this be cut in the rock forever, that his faith be perpetuated:

> I know that my Redeemer lives,
> that at last He will stand upon the earth;
> though my skin is flayed and destroyed,
> from my flesh I shall see God.
> I will see Him on my side;
> My own eyes shall behold Him, no stranger.
> (19:25–27)

"But my heart faints within me" (19:27). Job is driven to a place so far from ordinary human life, from human happiness, from all ordinary community of understanding, that only one Being can hold him up, only one impossible hope—and even here he faints. Eternity barely holds the just man up: my own eyes shall behold him. The Vulgate makes its point even more vulgarly: "I will be surrounded by my own hide again, and in my flesh will I see God" (19:26): this flesh, these bones, my own hide shall see.

There is a long history of debate among scholars about the significance of Job's speech here, as in chapters 14:7–17 and 17:13–16. The dispute is whether Job, driven to the extremity we see, finds the first seed or the last shard of the broken image of God where his misery gives him the only opportunity to look: whether looking straight at death he sees the glint green of resurrection. There are wise and careful Christians and Jews on both sides of the debate, and all the ancient texts are corrupt—in some places (particularly here in chapter 19) no two manuscripts seem to agree about anything. All our verbs are questionable. This, too, is a true revelation. Perhaps the original—if we can speak of such in a story that has its roots in an oral culture—was too incredible even to be set down correctly once. Aquinas, as wise a reader as God is likely to make, shows how the whole debate is between a man whose faith in God at the extremity of human experience leads him to see and hope for resurrection and the more materially comfortable comforters who neither need nor seek any such thing. Yet among the Fathers, Chrysostom argued against Job holding an affirmation of resurrection, laying these verses in 19 against 14:12ff ("So a man lies down and rises not again"). But chapter 14 is almost a debate between a Sadducee—who does not believe in resurrection (14:12)—and a Pharisee ("thou wouldst call, and I would answer," 14:15); it raises resurrection as a *question*: "If a man die, shall he live again?" (14:14)—and that text, too, is corrupt.

Contemporary commentators seem almost embarrassed to accept these verses as prophetic—as though *Job* (given the *Sitz-im-Leben* of the text) must not be seen even to approach this debate and this (shall we say?) offensive teaching, this proleptic anagogy of our coming life in Christ. But Augustine argued that what a sacred text means is everything true that it can mean, and some of those truths may not have been known to the author, and of the Old Testament it seems certain—if what it says is related to something which comes later which makes everything new without destroying it—some truths it contains can, necessarily, *only* be clearly seen by the actual events which followed. If one is only willing to read a text in light of its community's likely understanding, it would be impossible for any word to be prophetic. Or for prophet to build on prophet. Prophecy, from being an act of God, becomes merely a genre of human literature. Such reading is a practice of methodological atheism. So Augustine, who considers that Job was neither a native Jew nor a convert, regards Job himself as a symbol that the people of God includes others than those who are called on earth "the people of God." It includes the outcast on the ash-heap beyond the walls of a foreign city, long before our common era. But the verb Job gives to the Redeemer is in the present tense, not the future; as God is the God of Abraham, Isaac, and Jacob—the God of the living, not of the dead, so he *lives*, Job says—not the Redeemer of those who do not yet live but will, nor one who is coming later: I know that my redeemer lives, that in my flesh shall I see God.

It should be clear at this juncture that to read this book

presuming neither Christian nor ancient Jewish principles of interpretation is, in fact, to presume *against both* Christian and Jew. There is a multiplicity of interpretations available at junctures like this, but such junctures are hard ones; for here, to say yes to one interpretation is to say no to all the others, and to say none of them is to say that the words are senseless. Reading such a book is revelatory of the one who reads; every reading is, therefore, confessional. Perhaps our response to God's word is every bit as revelatory about us as is our response to suffering. Perhaps, then, in order to raise the right and true meaning or meanings from this text we have to be driven as Job is, not to the margins, but to abjection, not just outside of happiness, but into the gate of death while yet living. And then, were we so good as he, we might also prophesy, or interpret this tongue's story, or speak wonders not credible to the general run, whose troubles and virtues are common. If it is possible for anyone to see more deeply into the will of God than another, it is fitting that it should be such a man as Job, like whom there is no one upon the earth. The sufferings of the just or the innocent are not to be gazed upon with impunity by sinners, that I am sure of. I do not have the right, either as a scholar or as a man, to sit on this question, and I pray not to be drawn for this jury.

JOB 20

Zophar's Second Speech

ZOPHAR HEARS JOB'S REBUKE (20:3)—that is, he hears
that it is a rebuke, but whether he hears the truth of the
rebuke seems questionable. That is, he really doesn't hear
the rebuke. For the conclusion of the second round of
speeches is a specification of the catechism with which
Eliphaz opened it, and, as he specifies the fate of the evildoers, Zophar approaches a shadow painting of Job.
Indeed, Job was exulting and joyful, in his wealth he
seemed to mount up to the heavens (20:5–6); if God said
there was no one like him upon the earth for justice, the
narrator has told us there was no one as rich as him either.
Zophar echoes the narrator's earlier remark "when they saw
him from afar they did not recognize him" (2:12) with his
"those who have seen him will say, 'Where is he?'. . . The
eye which saw him will see him no more" (20:7–9). When
the mighty have fallen so far, they are not recognized—
even when you pass right next to them. Job has become as
unrecognizable as the once hale and happy evildoer Zophar
imagines. Zophar thereby implies that Job's wealth was not
accumulated justly, that he has now given back the fruit of
his toil, and from the profit of his trading got no enjoyment because

> He has crushed and abandoned the poor,
> seized houses which he never built.

[And] because his greed knew no rest,
he will not save anything in which he delights.
(20:19–20)

The lightning of the heavens which destroyed his flocks
and the storms which crushed his children in their houses
reveal (*ex post facto*) his iniquity, the very earth rises up
against him:

The offspring of his house shall be exposed;
he shall be pulled down in the day of God's wrath.
This is the wicked man's portion,
the heritage he is appointed by God. (20:28–29)

Job has this portion and heritage; therefore Job, evidently,
is just such a man.

It is, however, revealing that Zophar began by confessing
that he heard in Job's speech "a censure which insults me"
(20:1), and, as he says, he answers out of the spirit of his
frame; hastily, his understanding is aroused. Zophar is perhaps the youngest of the group of three counselors, for
throughout the discussion it is clear that evil is and remains
only an intellectual problem for him, himself untouched by
suffering. Job's accusation (19:22), that the comforters are
unjust pursuers (or perhaps worse—rapists of a prisoner of
war), causes Zophar to flame up into the most direct and
damning accusation against Job so far. Apparently, an insult
to his own justice and understanding will not be taken
lightly, and the suggestion that the wrath of God might
rightly fall upon him is anathema. The most militant
theodicide clearly thinks himself to be in the right before
God and right to pursue Job as if God; it is his self-justifica-
tion that flares out at Job—this is the spirit that gives him a
reply. We have seen this spirit before. He seems to be every-

where on earth. He dries up streams of oil, and his work dams up torrents of milk and honey (20:17). But Zophar allows us to picture what we must not be lest we cause life to become desiccated: not keep all the sweet things in our mouth, nor swallow everything given, for such fullness becomes poison inside (20:15), though it may taste as sweet as that wickedness we keep hidden under our tongue. Thus we become the one Zophar describes: "When he abounds to overflowing, he shall be brought into straits, and nought shall be left of his goods" (20:23). Even our goods will not be good for us.

JOB 21

Job's Response

JOB ASKS THAT his comforters pay attention—that would be solace enough—and then begins with a rhetorical question: "Is my complaint against man?" The answer, the rest of his speech makes clear, is a reverberate "no," and he expects that if they understand this they will clap their hands over their mouths in horror. The problem is for God; the solution is not in their ken. That they don't realize this is exactly why he is angry—and why should he not be impatient (21:4)? So he tries once more. The problem he wishes them to see is now not his own particular suffering, but the state of the world—particularly if their view of God's purely temporal rewarding and punishing is true:

> Why do the wicked go on living,
> grow old, even get richer?
> Their children in their presence...
> their homes free from fear.
> His bull sires without fail;
> his cow calves with no loss. . . .
> They pass their days in prosperity,
> and quickly go down to Sheol.
> Though they say to God: Be gone!
> We care not to know Your ways.
> (21:7–15)

On *Job*

Job's complaint is so strong and straightforward that some scholars think a troubled scribe may have added some verses, perhaps to calm his own fears as he copied these words; as if he is afraid, in copying, that God will misunderstand and take them as the scribe's own thoughts. So, for example, a line after what was just quoted, just before Job turns to tighten the problem, we read:

> Their prosperity is not in their hand;
> I am far from agreement with the wicked. (21:16)

But Job himself has said this before, and it is a universal moral truth; we need no editorial interpolation from a copyist. The second half of Job's speech begins with what he thinks, in all justice, *should* happen (18–21)—and in this he agrees with the position of his interlocutors: "May God not store up misery for His children; let his own eyes see his calamity" (21:20). But that roll of his speech (17–27) is broken again by what many modern scholars think may be a wondering scribe, originally, perhaps, in the margin:

> Will he teach God knowledge?
> Will he judge even the Most High? (21:22)

At least once, then, Job was heard—or maybe twice if they are two different scribes. These scribal inbreakings (if that is what they are) give some food for thought. There is something marvelous about this scribe, that he takes what he is reading so seriously. He is afraid to even write what those who sin truly are saying: "We do not wish to learn your ways. . . . What profit have we from prayer?" (21:15). He seems to feel that Job is going too far in the heat of his complaint against God's running of the world; as if he must answer the complaint of Job in his own voice, with his own hand. I imagine that such a one has not suffered much and

116

yet knows something of his imperfection. The happy life of the wicked touches more of his life than Job's suffering; so the description of this unmitigated happiness in which he shares reads like the most terrorizing condemnation.

Who reads so seriously now? But then, living in an age when, if a book was saved, it was saved by the person who wished to save it by copying it word for word, I suppose one would be more serious about one's reading. It is taking a serious part of your life to copy it out. Why copy it out if it does not speak to you of your life? And now, look what blessed Job's speech hints at… The printing press, like the copy machine or the internet, increases geometrically the production of babble, but wisdom remains what it always has been, something each person must copy over word for word in his own voice, with her own hand. It takes a serious part of your life to copy it out. That is too easy: copying a book is not what is at stake for this scribe. More likely it takes all of one's life to copy wisdom word for word in one's own voice and hand.

The first interruption (21:16) almost makes Job's complaint worse: Indeed, if the prosperity of the wicked is not in their own hand but in the hand of God, isn't that worse? For isn't God's injustice multiplied if the happiness of the wicked is not only not in their own hands, or not merely due to a *Deus absconditus*—a deistic excusing absence of God's working in person on his world—but in the divine hand itself and given by Him to the wicked? But the scribe, after saying this, remains far from agreement with the wicked, as if he would not accept happiness under the condition under which the wicked man has it—that he had told God to get lost, that he had said, "I care not for your ways" (21:14). This scribe seems to me to have touched the deep root of Job: that to live in all of the good things of the world, surrounded by children and wealth, and to die

> at ease and contented,
> his body full of fat and supple
> to the moist marrow of his bones (21:23–24)

would be, perhaps, the most terrible and frightening thing. Like Richie Rich dying in his sleep. The daring of this thought should give us pause: it is as if happiness itself—children, wealth, ease, in a word, prosperity—are insufficient for the man. As if they might all be nothing by comparison with this: to know God's ways. The scribe seems unwilling to speak the word—Be gone!—*even if Job's complaint is true*—that the wicked do indeed prosper—for he looks squarely at Job's charge, he increases its terror, for "their happiness is not in their hand" is a double-edged sword, and yet he remains far away from agreement with the wicked. He has, however, seen the horror Job paints. Here is perhaps the place to point out that Job's picture of the happy wicked echoes a view we have heard elsewhere in the book, for these evildoers ask, "what profit do we get if we pray to [God]?" (21:15). But this question, implying that the reason for serving the Almighty is profit, expresses Satan's view; and that expected profitable result—prosperity—if not precisely and openly that reasoning, seems to be shared by Job's friends.

Perhaps the first interruption is not really an interruption, but Job himself saying plainly what he sees, and what the prosperous do not see: their prosperity is not in their hand. Though they think they are in control of the world and all its goods, he sees the truth—just as he saw it when he himself was prosperous: "the Lord gives, and the Lord takes away, blessed be…" Job sees that the prosperous are in the jaws of a terrible delusion. They think their prosperity is in their own hands, and with this he is far from agreeing. They have prosperity but do not recognize its utter contingency, so have no relation—certainly not gratitude—to the giver. The horror of so great a delusion concerning one's own power and concerning what is the greatest good of and in all goods is what the speaker gives voice to.

The second interruption voices a somewhat different reaction; this scribe is shocked not at Job's story of how the world works, but at Job's *hubris*—for the second half of Job's speech, into which he breaks, seems to be just what the scribe says: Job's attempt to teach God justice. And this is just like the comforters, who are missing the real critique. It is not that Job is trying to teach God what justice requires, but that he is trying to get his friends to see that their materialist idea of God's justice has no empirical basis. Listen, he says, and consider these questions:

> How often is the wicked's lamp snuffed,
> or destruction come upon them?
> How often does He portion them pains in his anger?
> Or are they made as straw in the wind,
> or chaff that the storm blows away? (21:17–18)

It doesn't happen. On the contrary, besides a happy life, a full family, and an easy death, they even get a grave with a view (21:33). The philosophy of the comforters is an illusion; the idea of divine justice ruling the world the way they say it does has no empirical basis.

But if the idea of justice has no empirical basis, then where, on earth, did we get it?

And now the horror of the first scribe (if it is that kind of

119

interruption) and his rejection of the wicked even in their utter happiness become more sensible—palpable almost. The wicked have missed the most important and obvious truth about justice: that justice itself is divine, for those who are just did not learn it here, they did not discover it or invent it, it came upon them and took possession of their hearts from a world we have not yet begun to imagine. The wicked imagine the world to be only what they see; to see some other power operating, some hand not their own ruling over things, is inexplicable.

Or, rather, the whole history of philosophy has attempted to explain it. For to say we did not learn the idea of justice here evokes, almost immediately, the shade of Plato, the great myths of *anamnesis* (recollection) and the eternal forms, of the preexistence of the soul and its winged-horse chariot once driven in the processions of the gods. What other explanation can fit? What story less absolutely strange and unbelievable can be given for this utter absurdity: to see a gift in the fact of being, or to desire justice even to one's own destruction? To think that there can even be such things—which no one has ever seen the like of!

Or, to attempt another philosophical narrative, perhaps one less offensive in our anti-Platonic and anti-poetic day, let us suggest that the activity of God inspires by mimesis the activity of every kind of creature, one of which has a mind; therefore that creature's most equitable act regarding its own soul is to contemplate God, even though this is to stake everything in the smallest and least capable part, a part which is useless for all the rest of life, accomplishing nothing: the secret of the unity of Aristotle's ethics and metaphysics. Or it is to notice that freedom first appears to the mind as the command known as the moral law, and then to discover that not even the laws of nature by which animal, vegetable, and mineral are moved could *be discovered* were it not for the freedom of the mind which recognizes this absolute moral law as its own principle: Kant, in a sentence. All these are ways of attempting to understand what Job hints at: justice is not a discovery the material or empirical world allows; it is freedom's recognition of the eternal, and it has no cause. It can have no cause except what is eternal. But then, what should we say of that prosperity which seems to be, in the lives of the wicked Job points out, the very substance of the world? Is it not a frightful smallness by comparison? A non-world? Is not that whole world too small for what is awakened in us by meditating on Job's sentence?

Why—is it, how is it that there seems to be a horror in the comment—"their happiness is not in their hands"? Let us consider how this gift is not in our hands. The animal clearly suffers pleasure and pain, contentment and disease, but can it be happy? The happiness of the wicked, which Job catalogues before this interruption, includes all the pleasures and freedom from pain we could hope for—even a quick and painless death (21:13). If variety of pleasures and freedom from pain are happiness, then an animal can be happy, and the wicked man is a happy animal, and Job unhappy in his hide. To say that "their happiness is not in their hand" is only to say, then, that it comes to them by accident, or through the indifference of the divine dice player. This is not a matter for horror, but simply the stochastic rule of nature—the regular form of animal, vegetable, and mineral accidentality falling in the shape we call natural law.

But the scribe sounds more horrified than Nature's playing at dice would warrant. It sounds like the scribe thinks the capability for happiness is itself something which has an extraordinary source, and here are the wicked surrounded by wealth, food, and children—in which they take, one presumes, a *more than animal delight*—but they do not see what power it is that raises them out of the sea of animal pleasure and pain, of mere subjection to the good or ill effects of nature's dice game, to this high, more-than-animal plateau from which even the sorrows of Job fall away. But perhaps for them it is not so—is not that even more horrifying? Is justice itself required for happiness, not in the sense that happiness is a reward accruing to it, but in the sense that only the consciousness of this divine act in one-self, which act arouses that desire the psalmist regularly prays into—to know the law of the Lord—this conscious-ness of the capacity for and the demand of justice, or per-haps the bare capacity to know justice, unconscious and working still, is the actual condition for the possibility of anything more than mere animal happiness. Therefore, constancy in the activity of justice is growth in joy. In every circumstance. Animals cannot know justice; therefore they cannot know joy—or horror; they have pleasure and pain, and prefer the former. But for human beings it is not like that. For us, not only is our prosperity not in our hands (as it is not for any animal), the very hands of the evil man are not his own; they are *hands*, not paws, because of another power present even in him.

We recall that Job awoke early to offer his sacrifice, lest one of his children forgot, momentarily, to be grateful; he probably knew it is difficult, while happy, while enjoying the pleasures of life, to remember that the pleasures growing so lushly around one are not themselves the happiness—for the animal in its aboriginal jungle knows not of this joy; the real root of happiness is not in the earth from which these pleasures spring, but from an entirely different capacity in the one animal which walks upright in Earth's garden. And so to forget that capacity, or its source, to lose it in pleasure, or throw it away, is utterly, utterly horrible. Only for an animal whose every cell is drenched and embued or taken up into this entirely distinct power can there be this entirely different thing—happiness, or misery—so far different from pleasure and pain that it is another world entirely. This upright animal is a man; and, recognizing the significance of his uprightness, the first scribe can see that all the pleasures accounted by Job as belonging to the wicked are indeed pleasures, "but I am far from agreement with them."

This is the singular thread woven through the fabric of man. A philosopher who does not come upon it is merely imagining, not thinking; or worse, he is lying. All our instruments agree. On the other side of each philosopher's story mentioned above there is this: injustice is forgetfulness, brutishness, madness, falling away from being. If there is this connection between that power, idea, or capacity which allows us to be just and recognize justice, and the exaltation of happiness over animal pleasure, then no unjust man can be happy, nor can anyone who must look upon injustice—in particular no one who must look upon injustice in himself. Teach us your ways, O Lord.

And now we touch upon the real reason it is difficult to face the suffering of others, and so why we attempt to avoid it, to seal ourselves away from—or seal the suffering away in—ghettos, hospitals, old-age homes; this is why we do not sign up for tours of the gutters of Calcutta, the cardboard shantytowns of Lima and Tijuana, or the barren mud-hut villages of Zaire, for we cannot wish to be happy when others are not; we feel the injustice even of having this wish, to say nothing of knowing it satisfied, and we wish to be defended from seeing it, and the best defense is not to look, though perhaps in the real world where we cannot long avoid it we must go further, to that defense offered by Job's visitors—to say (or at least think, consider, entertain the probability...) that the suffering deserve it. Only then can we rest easy under the weeping of others. And so even the accusation of Job's comforters is a sign of something divine having happened to them. And of them displacing it.

And so, we might begin to see that here the deepest horror of Job touches the joyous certainty of the Beatitudes. For the horror of Job, and the horror of the scribe who first breaks into this chapter, is horror at injustice—at its affront to the very presence of the divine in man. The horror in the recognition of the scribe is not possible to a creature subject only to pleasure and pain, but only to one in whom there is something more divine. This recognition is certainly not learned here—among these rocks—where there is nothing unusual or untoward in the distribution of suffering or sunlight or rain. This horror can only arise in a creature who already partakes of something else, for to recognize injustice with horror is to be certain of something far higher already active in oneself. *Therefore,* blessed *are* the weeping, and the mourning, and the sorrowfully afflicted, and those who hunger and thirst for righteousness, for what cries out in them is an act of God. The divine is already at one with them, or they could not cry out in anything except pain, and Job does cry out in something more than pain. "Blessed *are* you when men reproach you, and persecute you, and say all manner of evil against you, lying against you for my sake" (Mt 5:11). Job is already blessed. Perhaps, in fact, another feast is toward in the happy kingdom where all the sons of God rejoice, and they speak of him there in tones of awe and wonder, and mark—as they would a signal fire—his glory.

Do you think the satan will appear?

JOB 22

Eliphaz's Third Speech

AT LAST it sounds like one of his visitors has heard Job:

> Can a man be profitable to God,
> even a wise man benefit Him?
> Is it good to Shaddai if you are just?
> His gain if your conduct is blameless? (22:2–3)

Eliphaz seems to be directly quoting Job's earlier question
(9:2) and, indirectly, the feeling behind questions like
why God would bring such a creature as man "into judgment with [Him]"—for "who can bring a clean thing out of
the unclean?" (14:3–4), and "if I sin, what harm do I do
[Him]?" (7:20). Eliphaz himself seemed to hear something
like this in the ecstatic nightmare of his first speech in chapter four (4:12–21). God's utter transcendence of human
good or evil seems, momentarily, to be a point of common
agreement. But this seeming agreement is broken in a way
that is perfectly perverse. For the next line runs:

> Is it for your piety He reproves you,
> and enters into judgment with you? (22:4)

And Eliphaz then begins the most direct and outrageous set
of accusations against Job that have yet been delivered; a
list of iniquities that has "no end," but of which Eliphaz
delivers only the major points: taking an unjust pledge
from a brother, stripping the naked, withholding bread and

water from those who hunger and thirst (22:5–9). He concludes the accusatory part of his speech with a story of the utter destruction of the evil ones and this reaction:

> The righteous see it and are glad;
> the innocent laugh them to scorn. (22:19)

Dante's Virgil taught him not to pity those who were justly condemned (*Inferno* XX, 27–30), but scornful laughter and gladness at the sufferings of others—even though the sufferings are just—seem to be going farther than a good person's feeling should allow, and perhaps even further than God's own love would permit if it is true that He wills not the death of the sinner. Eliphaz's conclusion does, on the other hand, agree with what Job has said several times—that the comforters are mocking him. Here the mockery rises to outright laughter—at least it should, if Eliphaz is serious about his charges against Job and about the proper response of the righteous, among whom he counts himself: Laugh him to scorn.

As with the previous chapter's presumed scribal interpolations, there is another stunning shift in the middle of this chapter, for in the course of his accusation of what Job and the wicked do, Eliphaz proclaims, "but the counsel of the wicked is far from me" (22:18). If the scribe, who—it seemed—fearfully and with trembling interrupted the immediately previous speech of Job to say that despite all the good things that come to them, "the counsel of the wicked is far from me" (21:16), is still copying, perhaps he now is struck with further fear at how easily his own words can come from the mouth of the self-righteous. The opening rhetorical questions had called up awe of Shaddai's transcendent holiness, only to turn—in one line—to mocking laughter of another being like us. Let the counsel of the wicked be far from me. Perhaps this, too, is a scribal interruption, and the scribe now sees that the wicked who ask "what can God do for us" (22:17) have the same relation to God as the orthodox Eliphaz, who is certain that God destroys whoever strays off the path. That view of God is that God is of interest to men only as a distributor of goods or evils, i.e., He is good as a means.

From his theological premises Eliphaz moves with inescapable logic to his moral conclusion in the person of Job, and this moralizing turns his emotions entirely outside the bounds of humanity: to laughter and scorn at suffering. We see the same thing happen to Augustine, when, believing the Manichean solution to the problem of evil, he refused to give figs to beggars for fear of trapping more light in the intestine darkness. It is dangerous for man to be touched by the living God. He must be entirely grasped by God or he will go far astray. Eliphaz, like the young Augustine, is touched; Job is completely grasped; God is not a means; the scribe continues his prayer, he too wishes not even to consider God as a means.

Eliphaz follows his accusations and moralizing result with a counsel of repentance which is almost comical:

> Put iniquity far from your tent;
> lay your gold in the dust,
> gold of Ophir among the stones of the stream.
> (22:23–24)

This, to a man with neither tent nor iniquity, who is himself laid penniless in the dust, and for whom to be laid amid the stones of a stream would no doubt be refreshing.

Finally, Eliphaz apparently ends by contradicting his

beginning, for he concludes with a reference to the transcendental attention paid to human sanctity, the moral earthquake it causes in God. So, supposing Job will change his ways to holiness, this will spark mercy in God for those who have it not:

When they are abased, you may order exaltation;
and the lowly among men He will save,
He will deliver one not innocent,
allow escape through the cleanness of your hands.
(22:29–30)

But of whom can this be true given Eliphaz's opening: can a man be compared to God, even if spotless? And who could that be? Aquinas says Eliphaz, by comparing Job's manifold wickedness or malice with his infinite or endless iniquity in verse five is distinguishing "the sins by which he has injured others" from "the sins by which he has omitted works of justice"[1]—some of which he goes on to detail. But who has not omitted some work of justice, considering, as Job has, that God never ceases to leave us alone even to spit? Who would have such cleanness that his hands could redeem others?

This suffering servant does not, in any case, laugh anyone to scorn—so much for that idea. But further, if God can allow the prayers of the just to deliver one not innocent, what becomes of the system of clockwork justice so often insisted on by the friends? From Eliphaz's last statement we should learn not to hold God to too stringent an accounting lest we constrain His mercy too. And what he suggests here, that the Holy One will accept the offering of

[1] Aquinas, *Literal Exposition*, 292.

one who puts his gold in the dust, or drops it as a stone in a stream, accounting the finest gold as no more valuable than dust and stream-stone, is so far ahead of itself that the mind boggles. Not the idea that the finest gold is as dust to divine holiness, but that the sacrifice of the just man will work salvation for the one who is not innocent. We have to rethink one of those opening rhetorical-seeming questions if this is true: Is it good to Shaddai if you are just? The answer now seems to be that the whole nature of the universe changes; God puts escape from evil for the unclean into the hands of the just. A mercy beyond comprehension in the hands of a mortal. Little does Eliphaz imagine whose hands will need to be grasped to save *him*.

While on first reading this chapter we may be disgusted with Eliphaz, we ought to be frightened, too. So many of his lines seem to resound in him from the choruses of the community of saints, yet he himself is so far out of tune. Should we laugh him to scorn? Or pray for his deliverance, that he may be allowed to escape, for he knows not what he is saying, or to whom?

JOB 23–24:17

Job's Reply

THIS MAY BE THE THIRD DAY of discussion between Job
and his visitors, since we are now in the third set of
speeches, and "even today," Job says,

> My speech is bitter,
> for his hand is heavy, despite my groaning.
> (23:1–2)

The friends have understood nothing, changed nothing,
heard nothing, discovered nothing; far from lightening the
burden of Job, they are like the hand of God continuing its
pressure—they are like God in adding to Job's burden, but
they are not like God in being a source of resolution. Job
cries out again to that resolving power, and again it is a
prayer I would not be able to join, still less to criticize:

> O that I knew where to find Him,
> that I might come to His judgment seat;
> I would lay my case before Him,
> and fill my mouth with arguments.
> I would learn what He would answer,
> and understand what He would say. (23:3–5)

Job expects that God would not come to him in power,
but listen, and reason, and acquit (23:6–7). There are two
things in this speech (23:3–10) that we should take note of:
First, Job has looked for God unstintingly, and while he has

found His works, he has not found their source; second, he expects that insofar as it is possible for a man to understand justice when God finally *comes to him* he will be weighed and found to be of the right measure. It seems clear that it is in the realm of the moral, not through seeking out the powers behind creation, that Job expects God to make Himself most understandable; it is the upright, not the great scientist, who might be able to follow His thoughts, nor would he need an interpreter or go-between:

> Through an attorney would He sue me?
> Nay, He Himself would give heed to me. (23:6)

He is not, it seems to me, arguing with God as the all holy transcendent God—in fact he admits that one to be totally beyond his ken—but he is considering God as someone much more intimate, one with whom, or by whom, justice could "be delivered" (23:7); and Job, in the imagery of that verb, is the laboring soul who would give birth to this seed which God Himself has planted. Job has looked for God everywhere, in every direction on earth, but He is nowhere to be found—that is to say understood, though Job knows that he himself is seen, and known, and tested (23:8–12). Job understands this much of God's justice: "He will prove me like gold" (23:10); He is doing so "even today" under the continuing pressure of his friends. "He knows my way."

Perhaps He is not done proving, and so Job's failure to understand God's causing and his realization of God's absolute transcendence in power and holiness lead him to say

> I am dismayed before Him;
> I think of it and recoil from Him.

> God has made my heart weak
> Shaddai has terrified me. (23:15–16)

To think that Job is merely terrified of God's power minia-
turizes the perspective, or dual perspective, Job has been
constant in: the awesome transcendent holiness of God,
who is beyond our measures of justice as He is beyond the
whole creation in power. Yet God, the human yet intimate
knower, in His sifting of Job would find him acceptable:
but how much more can He test him with? "My courage
fails" (24:16). Job's courage fails considering how much further God's holy power reaches (which his mind cannot
reach), but what he has already borne... I, who have not
suffered, and am not like Job, prefer not to contemplate
this matter too closely. Must we all face such intimacy?

Job begins the next chapter returning to the other side of
his bifocal vision of God, wishing God, like a king, would
set times for judgment, that his friends might bring their
cases before Him (24:1). Then he looks at the world and
sees in detail, again, that God seems not to be there:

> The wicked move boundary marks,
> they seize flock and shepherd.
> Orphans' asses they drive away,
> and they take the ox of the widow. (24:2–3)

They impoverish the poor ever further, make them reap
and press oil and wine while thirsty and hungry and naked;
the poor clear the fields of the wealthy and lie down in
them at night without shelter.

> And the murderer rises in the darkness
> to slay the poor and the needy;
> in the night he is as a thief.

The eye of the adulterer watches for twilight
saying, "no eye will see me."
...
In the dark they dig through houses,
and by day they shut themselves up,
for they know not the light. (24:14–16)

And after this last description of the evil in the world, we begin to lose track of who is speaking, and every translator and scholar begins editing and adding to a text that is obscure wherever it is not corrupt. As the world is, so goes the text—"and God sees nothing to blame" (24:12).

JOB 24:18–27:23

The Dialogue Continues

LIKE THE BEGINNING of *Hamlet*, the staging of *Job* now becomes completely shrouded in fog; voices are heard, but to whom do they belong? Do they mock and mimic one another or does each speak on its own accord? And how many speak? Who's there? And where? There is not much scholarly agreement here.[1] However smoothly some translations read, the original texts are full of lacunae, grammatical lapses, broken lines. Unlike Shakespeare's play, there is not yet a command cutting through this land of fog and shadow: "Nay, answer me!" Not yet.

---

[1] For example, Anderson in *The Interpreter's Bible* suggests the following division: 22:1–30 (Eliphaz); 23:1–24:17, 24:25 (Job); 25:1–6, 26:5–14 (Bildad); 26:1–4, 27:1–12 (Job); 24:18–24, 27:13–23 (Zophar); cf. 888 and discussion *ad loc*. The *Jerome Biblical Commentary* suggests 23:1–24:25 (Job); 27:7–10, 13–23 (Bildad); 26:1–4, 27:11–12, 2–6 (Job); 25:4–6, 2-3, 26:5–14 (Zophar). *The Anchor Bible* (Pope) suggests 22:1–30 (Eliphaz); 23:1–17, 24:1–3, 9, 21, 4–8, 10–14b, 15, 14c, 16–17 (Job); 25:1–6, 26:5–14 (Bildad); 27:1, 26:1–4, 27:2–7 (Job); 27:8–23, 24:18–20, 22–25 (Zophar). The intricacies of Pope's replacements are too busy for a copyist who wishes to make Job more agreeable to the wisdom of the day, but his larger breaks and identifications sound psychologically— that is, poetically—right to me. In any case, as future notes will show, I am not insisting on the division of speeches which follows, but suggesting a way of keeping the book's strongest formal feature: the call and response of triple dialogue.

On *Job*

But the very debility of the text might be a sign that a storm is brewing, that we have come to the edge of human understanding; perhaps it is already upon us, though we know it not. This shattering is a symptom. The generations of scribes who fought with this text while copying it seem to have fought particularly hard here, near the end of the lovers' quarrel between the just man and God—if that is what it is—or between the just man and some distant friends who echo at times the instigating spirit of Job's torments. The text makes some sense distributed to speakers as the RSV has it, but all of the formal structure the dialogue has thus far maintained is destroyed in that editing. Those formal structures are to be destroyed further with the unattributed psalm in praise of wisdom (chapter 28) and the sudden entrance of the heretofore unmentioned Elihu (chapters 32–37) before the heavens break open. Elihu is completely overlooked in God's final command (42:7); clearly his voice is late and perhaps rather carelessly added, as many contemporary scholars think. But before we get to that textual difficulty, or the question of the psalm, there are the considerable textual problems of this section.

Against the RSV's abandonment of the heretofore regular strophic and antistrophic structure of speeches, Pope's Anchor Bible radically rearranges the text to continue those more obvious formal features. It seems to me that it goes further in breaking and rearranging the received lines than is necessary to keep both sense and structure. The breaking and inserting of lines goes much further than I think it likely that a thoughtful religious scribe, or a plausible textual accident, would go in changing the received texts to accord with what he can understand. I think that such changes as a later scribe would make must have had to him at least the appearance of accidental miscopying, of skipping whole lines or sections on the part of a previous scribe. In short, the wholesale rewriting Pope suggests seems excessive.

In what follows I offer a more moderate editing; repairing, I hope, some ancient scribe's fearful, or merely accidentally broken, redaction. I do this with some trepidation, for however philologically inaccurate his text was Thomas Aquinas offers an explanation for the formal difficulties of this part of the text that is not without merit as an explanation, even in these days of form and redaction criticism. Noticing the absence of Zophar between chapters 26 and 27 he says, at the opening of his exegesis of chapter 27, that Job paused for Zophar

> to respond according to his usual custom, but since he was silent, as if convinced [by Job's previous speech], Job takes up the speech again and shows by another reason that it is not contrary to divine providence if bad men prosper in this world and good men suffer adversities. Hence the text says, "Job also added this," namely, after no one responded to him.[2]

But perhaps it is not Job speaking.

Bildad's Third Speech? (25:1–6; 26:5–14)

Eliphaz's secret whisperer (4:12–19; cf. 15:14–16) is perhaps heard by Bildad now, and the thought almost takes him out of the dialogue; his last speech is a psalm to the divine order, a recognition of unknowing and distance. In any

---

[2] Aquinas, *Literal Exposition,* 323 ff.

other context his beautiful series of distich lines would long since have become as well remembered as any of David's; and the breaking of it, and separation into different chapters with a four-line interruption by Job is, at least, a sin against poetry. That the usual translations make chapter 25 a chapter of only six lines is a confession to every reader of the brokenness of the original manuscripts. The cure to this break seems most obvious, and I will take the Anchor Bible's reconstruction for granted. Pope's translation of this poem is perhaps his best work as a translator of *Job's* poetry; it is, in any case, stunning. Here is the first half:

> Dominion and reverence are his;
> he imposes peace in his heights.
> Is there any numbering his troops?
> On whom does his light not rise?
> How can a man be just before God,
> one born of woman be clean?
> Even the moon is not bright,
> nor the stars clean in his sight;
> how much less man, a maggot,
> the son of man, a worm! (25:1–6)

> The Shades beneath writhe,
> terrified are the waters and their denizens.
> Naked is Sheol before him,
> perdition has no cover.
> He stretches Zaphon over the void,
> suspends the earth on nothing. (26:5–7)

Bildad's reminder that God's dominion is all-embracing, that His light rises on all, that all is uncovered—living and dead—is a response to Job's complaint about the evildoers working in darkness (24:13–17), but then he breaks off. He sees that before God there is no darkness, and so he does not make the usual turn to punishment, but to the glory of God, and to the terror which must come upon even the dead at having no cover from divine vision. If the earth itself stands on nothing, what does a man made of that earth imagine he can stand on?

> The pillars of heaven tremble,
> stunned at his rebuke. (26:11)

The whole psalm does not just stand together, it sings; and at the close it returns to the whisperer Eliphaz heard in the first dialogue and foreshadows what must have been the original poet's fast-approaching conclusion:

> Lo, these are but bits of His power;
> what a faint whisper we hear of Him!
> Who could attend His mighty roar? (26:14)

It is almost as if Bildad sees that even his own earlier spoken idea of retributive justice is but a badly heard whisper, or the misconstrued implication of a shattered and shattering dream. Indeed, if no man born of woman can be clean before God, what has all this business about the just punishment of Job been about—is it just a preface to what will be done to those less than Job, famous for his ways? Unlike Job, but like his elder Eliphaz, Bildad cannot hold to God's power and His justice in the same speech; and perhaps now, in his own speech, he begins to hear his condemnation. He cannot, as Fr Gutierrez would require,[3] be both prophet and mystic at once. It would be fitting for him to be silent hereafter. And so he is.

---

[3] See note on page 95.

On *Job*

Job's Response
(26:1–4; 27:1–7)

Between Job and Bildad in this section we seem to see almost an exchange of vital fluids. Each seems to have finally taken something from the other, losing or hiding something we thus far have considered their own. Though Bildad's praise-song has echoed elements of Job's own speeches, Job's response here is as excessive in its mockery as Bildad's speech was uncharacteristically unaccusative. But Job is also uncharacteristically short, as well as sarcastic, and still responding as if to accusation:

> What a great help you are to me,
> poor, weak man that I am!
> You give such good advice,
> and share your knowledge with the foolish!
> With whose help have you spoken,
> who inspired your speech? (26:1–4)

> As God lives, who refuses me justice,
> Shaddai who has embittered my life,
> so long as I have breath,
> while God's spirit is in my nostrils,
> my lips will not speak falsehood,
> nor my tongue utter deceit:
> I will never say you are right;
> till death I will not renounce my integrity.
> My innocence I maintain;
> my heart gives me no reproach.
> May my enemy be as the wicked,
> and my opponent as the unjust.
> (27:1–7)

The first four lines can be read as irony—or, perhaps more likely, biting sarcasm. Job seems so angry that he, it seems, has not heard that Bildad's last speech contained, as it seems, no accusation. His innocence has not been brought into question at all; nor has his integrity been questioned. Bildad's line "How can a man be just before God, one born of woman be clean?" (25:4) is something Job himself had implied in his previous speeches: "I am dismayed before Him; I think of it and recoil from him. God has made my heart weak" (23:15–16) and earlier: "If I sin, Thou dost mark me... / if I am righteous, I cannot lift my head" (10:14–15). *We* know better of Job's standing (on God's own description) as compared to others born of woman, but that is, after all, God's imputation—of which only the omniscient have knowledge.

Perhaps Bildad meant the line as an accusation, but, more charitably (as this proposal for division of the speeches runs), we could say that he has simply denied the claim of Job's previous speech that the wicked are not seen in the darkness and escape without fear. Near the end of these long discussions, he finally sees that things are truly otherwise: even the dead are uncovered. Bildad, in fact, seems to have come to the point of realizing that the enjoyment the wicked may have is not truly enjoyable, for they are not aware of how the world really is—under God's eye—even to the depths of the underworld. As his interlocutors' speeches seem not to have touched him, so Job's terrible oath here does not touch his most recent interlocutor (if indeed Bildad has not, in his last speech, reproached Job or taken up the usual cudgels of enmity). Further, Job's closing curse on the wicked ("Let my enemy be as the wicked..."

[27:7])[4] requires his own most recent picture of the invisibility of the wicked being wrong, and it almost requires that he think the position of the interlocutors up until Bildad's speech (to be taken up again, perhaps, and finally, by Zophar) correct: that their punishment should be direct and visible—*as in God it is.*

One line of what follows (which this reading will attribute to Zophar) might make this point concerning how things of the wicked really are: "He builds his house as of cobwebs" (27:18). Thus Job, in holding to his innocence, remains in God, that is, maintains his love of justice so entirely that his heart gives him no reproach. He knows his is the one true house, for his house is God's; the other is cobwebs. This reversal of characterization—if Bildad is not accusing, and Job is yet feeling accused—expresses how the constant pain of Job's illness and the ever-increasing complaints of his friends have driven him to the brink of paranoia. He is about to break into madness, for he hears accusation in Bildad's psalm of praise to God: if the world is supereminently the Lord's—who is supereminently just—then suffering must be deserved. But that may well not have been Bildad's implication in that last speech, nor even the direction of his thought, for he considers that even the stars are not clean in His sight. Perhaps Bildad was hearing the whisper of Him who is coming: who suspends the earth on nothing, for whom even the stars are of questionable brightness.

So, from the other side, the other element of this peculiar

---

[4] And perhaps 27:8–10, 13–21, as the Confraternity translation, for example, reads these as parts of Job's reply to Bildad. But then Zophar gets no final speech in this edition.

double star, the constancy of Job—if not exactly his patience—has perhaps led Bildad to see deeper than the talionic law he expected the world to exhibit. The world does not exhibit it; nonetheless it is already true: "The netherworld is naked before Him and Abaddon has no covering" (26:6). Perhaps that Job does not break under the onslaught of death, disease, and accusation has been a sign to Bildad, and one he reads, at last, not incorrectly. Perhaps Job's constancy has worn through to him. It is not something Job *says* that Bildad considers, but the mystic whisper which came to Eliphaz and might well have been wafting through the entire discussion—approaching now its hearable conclusion. For Bildad has come to consider that the greatness and power of God might almost require Him to hide His justice from man, since not even the moon and the stars are sufficiently untainted (25:4), nor even the light originally divided from the darkness (26:10) sufficiently pure that when He approaches the pillars of the sky do not tremble with fear. What then about man? (25:6).

But if Bildad has seen, or heard this, and *therefore* becomes silent, he has come part of the way to seeing Job, part of the way to a correct understanding of God. Perhaps it will take God's own action to bring him any farther: the action and argument of the just man is insufficient for Bildad's complete recreation.

Zophar's Third Speech
(27:8–23; 24:18–25)

Zophar does not seem to have heard any whispers. He breaks right in upon Job's concluding curse, without allowing the poet a chance even to give him an introduction. He is quick to get back on the high horse of talionic rhetoric:

What hope have the impious when cut off,
in the hour when God takes their life?
When trouble comes
will God hear their cries?
He should have delighted in God
and called upon him at all times.
Let me teach you how great is God's power.
Behold, you yourselves have seen it.
Why waste yourselves in empty words?
(27:8–12)

And so he sallies forth on what has been the usual reign of terror: Job's present calling on God is useless, has been useless, and will be useless. It seems to me quite adequate to Zophar's didactic rhetoric to think that the long-skipped-over conclusion to chapter 24 (18–25) fit originally here. Even though some of the verses are quite corrupt, it moves in just the tone with which Zophar begins, and ends with a trap and a question, daring Job to step into it:

He lures the mighty with his power;
he rises and he trusts in life.
He gives him security on which he relies
but His eye is ever upon him.
They are exalted a moment, and are gone,
laid low and gathered up like the grass,
like the stalks of grain that are cut down.
Or who can confute me?
Or prove that my words are not true?
(24:22–25)

After this, Job's conclusion (chapters 29–31) would naturally follow—as most scholars think happened in the original text, laying out his final defense and confuting at least the literal reading of Zophar's speech. For in that last speech, Job takes the trap, turns it inside out, and drops it on Zophar. Job has relied on God, not life, and he has been exalted *and* laid low. What Zophar has said might be true of us, who are less constant in both our reliance and our gratitude, but it is not so of Job, as we know from the beginning. After Zophar's final trap is broken (as we shall see shortly), it would be fitting for him, too, to be silent. I present this arrangement as a plausible hearing of these very mixed and difficult voices. And into that silence comes God Himself. This organization keeps the formal structure the poem so far has exhibited and, so far as I can tell, brings verses of a voice together without too much emendation and redaction. Were I copying the book on my own time, knowing it should be my only source hereafter, I might copy it so, yet footnote what the seemingly bolixed source said, for perhaps at another time the old order would make sense. It seems, however, that numerous generations—millennia—of scholars[5] have not found it to make sense in whatever order—or have found it, at least, to be problematic in all. Be that as it may, this arrangement makes poetic and prayerful sense to me.

[5] And for most of those millennia footnotes did not exist; one copied as one could understand—grammatically, symbolically, poetically, theologically—and all one's weaknesses had room to appear. *De me fabula narratur.*

JOB 28

The Wisdom Canticle

THERE IS DEBATE about the provenance—sometimes argued to be Egyptian—the authorship—same poet? Older independent work?—and speaker—Job? One of the friends? Or choral interlude?—of this chapter. Since it lies before Job's final justification, from which the original poem no doubt broke to God's response—the Elihu speeches (32–37) being almost universally considered a later interpolation—if the original author was ever going to step into his tale more directly, it would have had to be here. This seems, at any rate, either an earlier interpolation than the Elihu speeches or part of the original poet's work. The question is important because we want to think about the sense this section makes; and for that we need to have some idea of who the speaker is, which also might orient us in a certain direction, considering whom the speaker is addressing.[1]

Perhaps I am overly influenced by Greek drama, to which it is unlikely that this poet had any connection at all (if in fact Greek drama is not altogether younger than *Job*), but this seems to me like nothing so much as a choral ode. In such cases, the poet, himself often choregus, breaks the

---

[1] Aquinas, like everyone I know of before the advent of modern source criticism, presumes the psalm is Job's. But the language of this poem is quite (and stunningly) distinct from that of the rest of the book.

plane of representation and speaks directly his mind—at least in Greek comedy that is the case. Perhaps it was once an independent, even liturgical, prayer or song, which the poet breaks into here (as Augustine breaks into psalms in his *Confessions*) to express the difficulty of his position: for he has reached the end of his argumentative powers. In any case, this chapter feels to me like it fits much more with the rest of the poem; the coming speeches of Elihu do not feel that way at all. If its language contains archaisms or Aramaisms, this is as much an argument for the greatness of the poet as for the fact of another voice redactively adding his own view to the text. This chapter of *Job* reminds me, in particular, of the famous second ode of *Antigone* (333–383), which is also about the distinction between the clever power of man's mind, the extent of his contrivances, and the reaches of wisdom that are outside such grasping, and devolve to man only through piety. Augustine echoes it in those passages of the *Confessions* where he asks all beings around him to tell him of God and they require him to seek higher.[2]

Even as it is, in its supposedly corrupt and unreconstructed state,[3] *Job* goes deeper than *Antigone*'s chorus, and it is not as conflicted as *Agamemnon*'s. For while Sophocles points out that human contrivance finds its limit in death, and piety is a city's protection against pushing its own contrivances too far, *Job* says of wisdom not only that "it is hidden from the eyes of all living," not only that the deep and

---

[2] See, for example, *Conf.* 7.11.17–7.13.19, 7.17.23, 9.10.23–9.10.25, 10.6.9–10.6.10.

[3] The *Jerome Biblical Commentary* (cf. 526) suggests an alternative arrangement of the verses to that of, e.g., RSV.

the sea do not know it (28:14), but also that the land of the Underworld and the great god Death can say only, "we have heard a rumor of it with our ears" (28:21–22). For Sophocles piety is the boundary of human contrivance, for Aeschylus wisdom comes alone through suffering, but for each it seems something we can live consciously and fully within, in accord with the city's festivals and nature's order.

But *Job* seems to be suggesting that all the pious practices of human beings, and even the knowledge of lesser gods— like Death—are barely superior to fiction, scarcely to be heard or trusted: For who can tell of the life of God? The deep does not murmur it unto the deep; nor does Death know it, nor do the rims of the world hold more than a rumor of it. This wisdom is still far beyond what Sophocles saw as the limit: "God understands the way to it, and he knows its place" (28:23). The Greeks have a rumor, the Jews a sublime fear:

> Fear of the Lord, that is wisdom;
> and to depart from evil is understanding. (28:28)

One might think, after reading this, that the poet himself does not know what God will say, if He answers. If he steps out of his poem briefly, as Sophocles, choregus, himself might speak to the audience, or like Augustine, frequently and in diverse books. Then each (Sophocles, Augustine, the poet of Job) makes this psalm his own, and in doing so he writes so that every reader makes it his or her own also; by mimesis we become the singer. We might imagine the original poet writing this interlude, and having come so far, wondering how his problem may be solved even by the intervention of God. He has driven himself to the point where only God can solve his problem—but he does not know how God can solve it. Still, we know what our part is: Fear of the Lord, that is, wisdom, and to depart from evil is understanding.

JOB 29–31

Job's Peroration
and Concluding Oath

LET US SAY THAT the poet of *Job* is writing five centuries before Christ, let us say that his main character is as patriarchal as any patriarch, and once owned vast wealth, a wealth which included large numbers of slaves; let us imagine all the pre-colonial, patriarchal, socio-economic determinants of the character and of the poet in full, and then let us listen to this speech and attempt to consider justice a culturally relative concept and virtue an effect of social embarrassment, or a mere empty variable subject to considerable socio-cultural caprice and interpretation. Let us try to read this merely as a cultural artifact, from a culture nothing like ours. That would protect us from what it says; but we can only hear what the inspiring spirit of this writer speaks by listening to Job's poetry as spoken today in our ear. And this is not at all difficult to do; he is a better speaker than our point-and-click age can develop, but his speech is not out of touch with realities we too would be involved in were we attentive.

Job remembers God's love and wishes for it, he recalls the friendship of God upon his tent (29:4), when by God's lamp he walked through darkness (29:3), and what he remembers of this love is not his own pleasures, but its enabling effect. When his steps were washed with milk and the rock poured out streams of oil, he was a conduit; a conduit so great that princes shut their mouths at his approach:

> Because I delivered the poor who cried
> and the fatherless who had none to help them.
> The blessing of the perishing came upon me
> and in the widow's mouth I was a joyful prayer.
> (29:12–13)

Like anyone of his class, he was recognized by his rich clothing, but Job's clothing made the noble tongue cleave to the roof of his mouth, for his robe was righteousness, and justice, and care for each:

> I was eyes to the blind
> and feet to the lame.
> I was a father to the poor,
> and I searched out the cause of the stranger.
> I broke the fangs of the unrighteous,
> and made him drop his prey from his teeth.
> (29:15–17)

Like a great tree Job's root went deep to the water of God and brought it up all night as dew for those thirsting above ground (29:19). They waited for him like the rain (29:23). Because of his piety (let us take that as the summary of all his virtues, since all virtues are powered by it) men listened to him; he chose their way, and dwelt like a king among his troops, like one who comforts mourners (29:25). Clearly, he was honored—but who should not honor him? Clearly, he had great power—but to what purpose does his arm turn? To comfort the mourning, to be eyes to the blind, to father the poor and defend the stranger. The honor was deserved, the power he had was power to do good, and he was unstinting. In his face the usual princes of this world fell silent.

But now they make sport of him (30:1), he has become their song and a byword (30:9), and his soul is poured out within him, and days of affliction take hold (30:16). Now he is like the vineyard its owner has abandoned:

> They break up my path,
> they promote my calamity;
> no one restrains them.
> As through a wide breach they come;
> like a tempest they roll on. (30:13-14)

Only this vineyard is a living, breathing, and feeling one, and recognizes some of those who he once fed and now raise their hooting cry over his affliction:

> I am a brother of jackals,
> and a companion of ostriches.
> My skin turns black and falls from me,
> and my bones burn with heat.
> My lyre is turned to mourning,
> and my flute to the voice of those who weep.
> (30:29-31)

In the worst of times a man might despair of mankind, or turn from justice for the sake of his life, but Job, though disgusted—and rightly—at the sore abuse of nature and man, does not turn so, and steadfastly refuses to do so, and swears so to God from the deepest abjection into which the satan can cast him. And what he swears to is stricter than the Old Law required, stricter than his society has heard rumor of, so strict that the sins his friends have imagined fall far beneath him, and he speaks from a mountain which has not yet been thought to be habitable. His law goes through the deed to the heart:

> I have made a covenant with my eyes;
> how then could I look upon a virgin?...
> If I have walked with falsehood...
> if my step has turned aside from the way,
> and my heart has gone after my eyes...
> If my heart has been enticed to a woman...
> (31:1, 5, 7, 9)

He calls down all the justice of God, as justice and patently deserved, if he has so much as looked upon a woman with lust, or let desire walk one step in the path of deceit. Who is there like him upon the earth? Even to the beginnings of sin he denies entry. For God walks with him always and considers each step of his ways.

He goes further: he claims that a slave can have cause against his master, and that the master must answer to the slave before the God who made them both. He claims the equality of men under God—and maidservants too. He teaches that the poor not only deserve enough to live on in health (have I caused the eyes of the widow to fail?) and in the community of the respected prince (or is the orphan to eat his morsel alone?), but claims he has withheld nothing that the poor have desired. Who can this be true of—and, from a position of power such as Job's was, who can be found to practice it? But Job has not trusted in gold, or any of the other false gods in which his society encourages worship, nor even let his heart be secretly enticed by them (31:24–27), constant though they must be in the marketplace. He has not rejoiced at the fall of one who hated him, nor have the homeless spent one night in the street, nor has

anyone not eaten his fill—not of leftovers, but of meat—
and at his own table. That he claims not to have hidden his
sins out of fear of the contempt of others does not imply
that he has sinned, but rather that the reason he has not
sinned is not vanity, fear of embarrassment and contempt,
or love of honor, but love of God from whom is all goodness. And if all this is not true, he says, let Adam's curse be
renewed upon him,

> let thorns grow instead of wheat,
> and cockle instead of barley. (31:40)

Let those of us who have not done likewise weep for
mercy, for we have sinned with Adam. We do not yet know
how to mouth the first syllable of such complete piety as
Job's. Job claims to have lived it, and to have lived it out of
love.

Who is there on earth like unto Job?

I said earlier that Zophar's last speech was a trap: he had
dared Job in saying that God had given the wealthy, like
Job,

> security on which he relies
> but His eye is ever upon him.
> They are exalted a moment, and are gone,
> laid low and gathered up like the grass
> (24:22–23),

but that he and they had come to depend on the goods,
keeping them as insurance, forgetting that goods are like
grass. He closed with this dare:

> Or who can confute me?
> Or prove that my words are not true?
> (24:25)

With Job's final speech the trap is sprung on Zophar:

> If I have, like a man, hidden my sin,
> Concealed my iniquity in my breast
>
> …
>
> Let the almighty write out the book,
> Let me carry it on my shoulder
> Or put it on me like a crown:
> Like a prince I will carry it
> And present myself before him. (31:33–37)

There will be no amen from me for this final prayer of Job's, nor will I look at Zophar to see if he blushes. And note that Job promises to "present himself" on the next feast day, with all the other sons and daughters of God. How may I come into this gathering?

God having written the book of Job's deeds and heart, will Job present himself carrying a heavy load on his shoulder? Or will it be an insignia of his office and will he be wearing a crown? Or will he present himself with both load and crown, nonetheless bearing it like a prince—a prince even among the sons of heaven?

JOB 32-37

The Speeches of Elihu

So these three ceased answering Job
because he was convinced of his righteousness. (32:1)

IT IS THOUGHT BY MOST contemporary scholars that the younger character who now speaks is the addition of some later scribe, some later reader and copyist who was troubled by the text he was spending his time on. Troubled because God's cause seems not to be adequately defended. This later poet-critic gives his character a long introduction, making doubly sure we know his full name, Elihu (He is my God), son of Barachel (God has blessed), his nation (the Buzite) and family (Ram), and his motive: that the silence of the friends at this point seems to allow the condemnation of God (32:4). But while that motive (though not, I think, the most reasonable conclusion to draw about Job's speeches) might be a good motive for speech, the writer of the Elihu speeches—having supposedly appeared after the original book was completed—must also not have found God's own speeches, which would have followed immediately here, to be adequately clear or sufficiently explicative. It is strange to think so, but so it must have been according to modern critical theories—even though the Buzite admits early on that "God is greater than man" (33:12). Apparently the writer found that even God did not answer well enough, and this later scribe is here to help Him bring out the main points. Aquinas considers that "this whole description is valuable so that he (Elihu) may be shown to belong to a historical event."[1] He considers that Elihu has been silent so long out of respect for his elders (as Elihu, in fact, says). Elihu, in any case, like the friends of Job, has theodicidal tendencies, as his speech was probably first inserted here by someone with a similar purpose. So there is also a bit of vainglory clouding his motives: "listen . . . and I will show you my knowledge" (32:10). Someone who would be, as it were, clearer than God, more forthright and perspicuous than He-Who-Is.

Having been given an introduction by his author-scribe, Elihu himself proceeds to take almost thirty lines to introduce his speech to his fellow characters (32:6–33:7), excusing his youth with his practiced patience and guaranteeing the worth of his coming speech to the wise by claiming an incapacity to control the inspiration which God breathes into him at Job's complaints and the current silence of his older friends. The scribe-critic of all the previous speeches, who is about to fold his speech into the revealed text, thereby folds himself into the speech of his character. Whether he is young or old we will never know, but he has, according to the scholars, come into the discussion later than the three friends; he is rightly a bit nervous about his interpolation, hence the several and long introductions. The repeated protestations and announcements that he is just about to speak are somewhat comical, but I think we must be thankful that the critic/poet/editor who was inspired to put these speeches here did so in this way.

We who live so much later in the history of God's people

---

[1] Aquinas, *Literal Exposition*, 366.

and are just such youths must be most especially thankful. For when I think of all the men and women who have read and commented on this book, studied it prayerfully and lived (or tried to live) in accord with its wisdom—Jews and Christians, the greatest saints and most learned rabbis, people so superior in wisdom, patience, and learning, to say nothing of their more particular moral excellences—people under whose merits I hope my sins will be hidden—it seems an act of *hubris* to attempt to read this book and think through it without having paid as long attention not only to the book itself but to its surrounding books, and to all those previous readers' comments and more importantly their lives. For many of those readers, perhaps the best, were not writers at all, or scholars, yet most, like Job and perhaps his friends, are older, wiser, and better. A real youth, who cannot yet have suffered much but feels that something more remains to be said—to Job, and to his friends—is almost just by his presence a bit of comic relief. As Elihu comes in late in the day, so do I, and every modern reader as well, whenever we approach the book, pick it up, read. Job and his friends are already there, the discussion just now (and still) going on (and thousands of millions of unheard interlocutors, who merely heard these words and kept them in their hearts), and we, late listeners—fit to swell a progress, young beyond all telling, more than a little foolish, perhaps even accomplished sinners, not nearly as novel or helpful as we might think in the face of terminal suffering—we too, like Elihu, are drawn into the discussion, and into the suffering of life which we bear—in one way or another.

So this later addition to *Job* is, in a way, comforting, for the heretofore unheard-of and much younger Elihu speaks, and as it were adds himself to the text—which all of us late readers do—saying he has the main point (33:8–11) and has to get out what he thinks on the matter. He looks a bit foolish, a bit full of himself, like he suffers a bit from the *hubris* he accuses Job of having, but he comes in anyway and stands there now in the text of the divine word—as do we. A somewhat ridiculous character (full of high sentence, but a bit obtuse); one who says what he thinks of the discussion, and though he is not as good a poet as the previous writer, nor sees so deeply, he is yet someone who says something worth hearing, and so we ourselves, taking his place in the story as it were, can hope to read meaningfully and think not unworthwhile thoughts in paying our fitful attention to the wisdom of *Job*. I, at any rate, here find my patron saint in the text—so far as he is a saint.[2]

While much of Elihu's speech sounds like the same arguments the comforters made—that Job's claim is that he is clean and sinless (33:9), and that claim is false, and so necessarily his charge that God has engaged in baseless persecution (33:10) is blasphemy—his argument does not, at least, start from the usual empirical premise of Job's suffering. He merely states God's world-arching justice as a fact and proves Job's deserts by his very claim to be just, which claim in itself Elihu finds offensive (34:5–7). Elihu also denies that God has failed to answer or speak to Job, against Job's complaint that God constantly refuses to appear and to answer.

---

[2] Wiesel, in "Job," says, "Elihu is the unworthiest character in the play. No wonder that, in some sources, he is identified as the reincarnation of Satan who used him to stage his own comeback" (131). Robert Alter, in *The Art of Biblical Poetry*, argues he is "an irascible, presumptuous blowhard" (113), though he also gives him credit for "something more than the rehearsal of formulas we saw in Eliphaz and Zophar" (114).

In fact, Elihu says, God speaks in different ways: "God speaks once" in creating the world, thereby instituting natural law as the created effect of the divine eternal law—"whether one perceives it or not" (33:14). "Therefore . . . far be it from God to act wickedly . . . nor can the almighty violate justice" (34:10–13). His original word instantiated it. Sometimes he speaks through dreams, and sometimes through suffering itself (33:15, 19). Job had admitted the first way of communication in 7:14, and had admitted the dreams God sent were fearful. Eliphaz, too, had had a fearsome vision (4:12–21). Elihu's point is that Job did not pay sufficient attention to allow the dream to "put an end to his pride" (33:17), so God had to take his conversation to the second method—continued suffering itself (33:19).

Elihu thinks that suffering is God's means of instruction, and the point is not—necessarily—that Job is a sinner (though he makes that accusation), but that suffering may be due him for the vanity of belief in the fruitfulness of his own good works: "If you are righteous, what do you give Him, or what does He receive from your hand?" (35:7). Job therefore multiplies his transgression with every word about his justice, and he is impious in clinging to it (34:35–37). Now this is a point that touches upon truth, but as with the ark of the covenant we must be careful how we touch it. Unlike what is true of myself and most likely readers, God Himself has said there is no one like Job, but Elihu implies that Job's claim of innocence is false and the mark of a scoffer (34:5–7), and then begins the usual paean that "according to the work of a man is he requited" (34:11).

Elihu's pretense of knowledge of Job's spiritual life every reader knows to be false. His theodicidal tendency leads him to judgment of his fellow man, as theirs did the three others.

An earlier phrasing, however, had suggested that suffering, like dreams, might be sent to keep a man from pride and so save him from the pit (33:17–18). So it *might* be his place to ask Job to consider whether his justice is his own gift to himself and his own work entirely—and about this it seems Job has not taken a stand—but, unfortunately, such an accusation is itself a mark of pride. Elihu concludes that Job has the satanic complaint: it is not profitable to take delight in God if there are no rewards. From an original insight— trust not to your own power in your good work—Elihu seems to have fallen to the usual level of Job's comforters: your work has been on the wrong side of the line. But we must not forget that the man he is judging is like no one else upon the earth; he has been upright, and we have no Pelagian exclamation on Job's part that he has been so through his own power acting alone. Perhaps his original response to suffering—the Lord gives—was meant to be all-encompassing: He gives not only the goods that are now lost, but also the power to do good and avoid evil, which very last power Job does not lose, even though his wife suggests that he throw it away: curse God and die. He avoids that evil.

But Elihu's point, that God has spoken and does speak to men, is better than the usual comforters' line. He seems to be saying that dreams to some and suffering to the more hard-headed each aim at keeping the good from trusting in their own righteousness, or trusting that their righteousness deserves a reward, while the dreams that may come in a calm sleep under the one word of creation might show unnoticed shadows from the busy and less attentive day. In the most poetic image of the first half of his speech he seems to imagine (33:23–25) that Everyman must leave even his good deeds as baggage at the station, and not pretend to

161

bring them before God, though, perhaps, an angel may speak in his favor, and sifting through the shipwreck of his life—perhaps not even of his life, but of the world—may come upon something which allows him to say, "Hold; I have some ransom for his release" (33:24),[3] and so he may not be swept bag and baggage into the pit.

If Elihu means anything different from the friends when he suggests that Job must entreat God's favor and confess his sin (33:26–27) and that doing so will be salvific (33:28–30), it must be this: that Job's sin was this one by which only the very good can be tempted—trust in their good works as valuable and worthy before God, pride in their fulfillment of the law, resting in the law and its fulfillment, not in God, whose greatness is the one source of law and so of all good, mercy, and justice. The speech, then, calls into question the entire project of the Old Testament, for it suggests that no one can rest there in fulfillment of the law, that even those *known to God as the just* would rest there unjustly. The least act of justice is God working through and in the just person.

If this is the right way to understand the passage about the angel who sifts through the flotsam of our lives, then what Elihu is mocking as absolute irreverence when he quotes Job's complaint "I am innocent…" (34:5–6) is not the usual comforters' idea that one who is suffering so much cannot be innocent, nor even, quite, the sometime touched-upon question whether a man can be justified before God at all, but that the speech itself is a confession of the sin of pride, and a sign of rebellion (34:37) against

---

[3] Perhaps an onion, as is suggested in Dostoevsky's *The Brothers Kara-mazov.*

the source of justice, and the holder of its reins (34:13–17). Since "all alike are the work of His hands" (34:19), all alike "perish on the instant" He forgets them. And since *to be* is itself an undeserved gift, complaining of injustice seems not to be plausible:

> If He is silent, who can condemn Him?
> If He looks away, who can find fault? (34:29)

Whatever we have we owe, since even our being is extravagant: "The Lord gives and the Lord takes away; blessed be the name of the Lord" (1:21). Further, if God were merely that perfect talionic justice the friends have imagined, we would have to forego His mercy—among the effects of which is our beginning in being at all. This last (we perish on the instant He forgets us) is a threat: suppose having borne chastisement a man might say, "I will offend no more"—but even then does God owe something to him (34:31–33)? A Job confident of his innocence might not fear such justice (though remember his sacrifices for his children), but in the context of the rest of the speech, particularly 34:14–15, it almost tells us that everything is mercy, "and what then can you answer?" (34:33). If everything—from the beginning—is mercy, then...

Even when Elihu does seem to claim that Job is a sinner, as Job's friends had, he sees more clearly than they did that the good and evil we speak of are merely human categories (35:6–8), so when human beings cry out either for justice or against oppression,

> He does not answer,
> for they are self-willed and proud.
> God does not listen to trivia,
> Shaddai pays no attention to them. (35:12–13)

The self-will and pride according to Elihu, then, must be in thinking that our good and evil are of import to God, whereas before God such speech is windy nonsense; the proper response to God's greatness is humility and gratitude. There is no right to be happy against him, for there is no right *to be*. Where the precedent cause is love, there is no cause, no charge justly taken against it. None even thinkable. To think there is is to deny the being of God, who is that creating mercy. It seems the case, however, that Elihu's prayer (again sounding like an earlier voice): "Let Job be tested to the limit" (34:36), was already answered; the proof suffered and given: the Lord gives, and the Lord has taken away; blessed be the name of the Lord.

I am not sure how much of this crosses Elihu's mind, or that his words prove the justice of his Maker (36:3) as he seems to think, or whether, in fact, such proving is hereby proven not to be a viable procedure in which to engage at all. We must speak of our justice vis-à-vis God in the same way we may speak of our being: dependent and generally dry wadis of the original river of righteousness. Elihu explicitly attempts to prove God's justice in the first half of chapter 36, but in doing so he steps into the same falsities the friends did, the same theory of immanent retribution:

> If they listen to Him their days prosper,
> if they do not listen, they die. (36:11)

> Avoid turning to mischief,
> for that is why affliction tries you. (36:21)

Moreover, this is precisely the rigorous and empirically visible justice Elihu had, it might seem, argued against, presenting all as mercy. He seems not to notice he has gone back on his insight.

So finally, this issue of the immanent justice of the world, and problem of innocent suffering that seems to contradict that divine justice even more than the happy lives of many sinners, for it contradicts even that opposed edge—mercy—hangs up this latest speaker, and his vision of it does not extend significantly farther than the others'. Or perhaps the inability of them all to get past this problem should make us, finally, aware of a fact, and make us think through this fact from a perspective less grand than *Defensor Dei*. The truth of the matter, and an escape from this error of universal retributive justice worked out by God in the world, which results in the interlocutors' universal conclusion that Job somehow deserves what he gets, starts not from the metaphysics of justice—with which, in any case, we are not perfectly familiar—but from what is more well known to us: that the first moving cause of innocent suffering is a human sin, or perhaps we should say a spiritual being's sin.

An obscure and quite uncertain line (34:30) is translated in Aquinas's Vulgate as He "makes the hypocrite reign because of the sins of the populace," which suggests to Thomas that the evil "prosper because of the sins of others."[4] This suggests a divine and exacting *lex talionis*, but I think the more accurate idea is that sin is a *wild* injustice; evil, then, is not a repayment for anything; it comes upon the person it comes upon (Abel, say) without expectation or warning, from out of the blue, just as everything has happened to Job. The sinful act does not carry its immediate evil effect into the sinner, the children of the sinner, or anyone connected with him, but first and most visibly into

---

[4] Aquinas, *Literal Exposition*, 389, 413 ff.

the wildly innocent—the innocent who have no connection to the sinner at all except the claim of common
humanity and the mercy of being: the clerk at the 7-11, the
schoolgirl on her way home, the homeless man under the
railroad trestle. But then the effects of this act, and vision of
this act, and the report of it, and the memory of it—let us
say the blood of it—where does that go? Into the earth.
And what then might it effect? Where are the pressure
points of the world's body that suddenly feel a gushing of
blood, a new and unexpected stress, an unmerciful pressure? Or what gears of the universe suffer a bloody slip-
page? Is the world just anymore? Can it run right? Can it be
made to do so?

And where did it start, really? Did the clerk at the 7-11 get
killed—by a youth his own age—because that boy had seen
someone else with more than he needed, while he went
hungry to school every day? Perhaps the first sin (more
cookies at lunch than anybody else) looked victimless, perhaps this was not the first…, or perhaps there is no such
thing. Sin opposes the mercy of being; should we not, then,
expect merciless things to be and to happen—perhaps even
more and more of them? And again and again. To set oneself, even for a moment, against the mercy of being—where
in all the universe, held in being by mercy itself, where
could such an intent and action show up? Anywhere. It is
out of sorts with all creation, it is against the law of all
being; it is wild. It wanders. "Here and there around the
earth." Shall we participate in this wandering? Well… and
so who is suffering it? And remember that Job rose early
every day to offer sacrifices, for "it may be that one of my
sons…" (1:5).

The theology of perfect retribution would have to deny

the wildness of not just the original sin, but any and all sin *and all its effects*, and it is just this wildness which has as its mirror image and direct result wildly innocent suffering. The defenders of God are wrong about God's justice because they are wrong about man's sin; they do not see its utter seriousness—the seriousness even of the smallest act, that its wilding destroys the ontological innocence of creation. This innocence no retribution can restore. How could it? There can be no perfect retribution, nothing can make up for it. Nor is it unlikely that, since we have so polluted creation, earth itself revolts at us: "By the sweat of your brow..." And therefore every sinner must submit to suffering knowing with certainty that no evil that he suffers, not even if he understands it as punishment, can bring the turning axle back to true. Job, too, suffers this; and suffering it is his proving faithful. To the innocent sufferer the sudden onslaught might well feel like the rock to Sisyphus, a crushing absurdity; but the rock is not put there by the cruel sentence of an unjust God, for as the rock is to Sisyphus, so is the sinner to his victim. That it falls upon anyone in particular is merely the wildness of sin. Job's interlocutors seem to think that the truing of the world's axle can and does take place in the world, that the world is—eventually—perfectly retributively just, that the wheels are trued even as the world spins on and we act. No; the world is groaning and cries out for its re-creation. Only that will answer: all things must be made new again.

If we are to love God for nothing—and it is the satan who suggests Job does not, but does so for the rewards—then the negative of the world in which such a picture may be taken is the senselessness of suffering. If suffering made sense, we could make sense of all the good as well; indeed we could make dollars with such knowledge, or at least save them. Job's visitors have not spoken rightly about Yahweh, and they have not spoken rightly about man. They have not spoken rightly about the world or Yahweh because secretly and perhaps unknown to them they have agreed with the satan's view: that goodness and justice are worth something: they earn something before God. That this view is a denial of freedom the Grand Inquisitor[5] makes clear, and as such it is a misunderstanding of man. The visitors have not spoken rightly even about the sinful man—who might be willing to pay for his sin, might be so bold as to say, "let come to me what may, I'll have it"—much less the just man, the man like whom there is none upon the earth.

What the just man may not have seen, and the sinner requested to be otherwise, comes plain in the suffering of the just and the innocent: that any sin is an attack upon not only innocence, but all creation's being. The interlocutors have not spoken rightly about Yahweh because they have not spoken rightly about human beings; in particular, they have not looked into the face of sin, which is faceless, while they have presumed it to have the visage of Job: but the face of sin is not a human face. We need not travel so many days to see into the face of sin. It is not pretty, and it is not Job's, and it is much closer to home. But, if we look, we should notice first of all exactly this: that sin's effects are wild: that is its face. It is not merely I who pay for my sins, or not just my children, but those children over there—living on the street in Lima, sewing shoes for sixteen hours a day in China, sold for a night in Bangkok. And like Job,

---

[5] I mean the character in Dostoyevsky's *The Brothers Karamazov*, who is himself a modern figure of Satan.

the innocent do not know why this rock falls upon them. This guilt is not purgeable, it is not able to be borne, and at times I near-despair of its ever being lifted. This is the proving of Job: in such straits he looks for God.

Who would not understand that quite different Biblical hero Samson? Who would not wish for his strength, having once seen the horrible wildness of what we might once have thought of as the smallest sin? Who would not understand his prayer to be crushed under the stones with his enemies, that is, with his sins, crushed among them—perhaps his only one—his exorbitant love for the twining hair of Delilah. The just man knows in his flesh what the sinner can only come to know by reflection—not on his own pains, but on the pains of the just and the terrors visited upon the innocent: the utter wildness of sin. For the rest of us it is not so wild. It is this that Job's terrible cry means to teach us who are not Job; for when pains and terrors come upon the sinner, when the breath is slowly crushed out of him by the crushing weight of the stones, he—we—can know, like Samson, from whom and why it comes. Job, however, does not know that weight, for whom or why he is bearing it; nonetheless Job says, "I know that my redeemer lives," and He will show him what part is his: he will know even as he is known. But until then... Samson, on the other hand, wishes to pay for his lack of obedience in his own hide; he counts this as the final blessing granted by divine mercy, an answer to his prayer: Let me be crushed with my enemies, let my sins and all their effects die with me. But even this is not sufficient for rectification. Not even this. For Samson and all the rest of us sinners were created good, and that has been lost. Has it been lost forever?

I do not think Elihu sees this point, but it is more likely

that he breaks off because he is aware he has stepped into the same contradiction as the others (36:22), and so begins his paean to creation's God (36:26–37:24). The author of *Job*, in any case, saw the storm coming; for the storm was already present when he began writing. In this last part of his speech, at any rate, Elihu and his poet/critic do well; and the poetry, undoubtedly inspired by the developing storm, reaches equality with the poem he has joined himself to. We should take hope in this fact too: that the inspired word can inspire even the self-contradictory and largely unpoetic latecomer, that is to say, the ordinary person, into a better state. And so the words of all men end in praise, and this supposed interloper takes up all the speeches and speakers into his conclusion:

> Therefore all people pay Him reverence,
> and all who are wise look to Him. (37:24)

I am, in reading *Job*, unconvinced that it is only in our century—after our holocausts of Jews and Kulaks, Armenians and Africans, Cambodians and Chinese—only now that theodicy is at an end, or ought to be. I am not sure that our century has a "revolutionary fact"[6] to tell us about suffering. As Dylan Thomas wrote, "After the first death, there is no other."[7] The large number can only be to attract our attention, for we are much less attentive, little given to examination of conscience in these modern days. And it is, after all, *our* large number. The large number is because we

[6] Emanuel Levinas thinks it does; "Useless Suffering," translated by Richard A. Cohen, in *The Provocation of Levinas*, R. Bernasconi and D. Wood, eds., 161.

[7] Dylan Thomas, "A refusal to mourn the Death, by Fire, of a Child in London," in *Collected Poems*.

have become so hard of hearing. But even in this regard I wonder if we might not turn it to being counter-productive, for now we seem to be able to point *out* the evil one, to give the faceless one a personal name and home country or tribe: "over there," "then," "those people." And, of course, "it can't happen here." We are tempted thereby to think the problem is clear and the solution obvious. We say, "never again, as there once," even as it is happening now and here.

This political and social scapegoating is something which was not hazarded in *Job*, though Job himself was unaware that the evil visited upon him had its source in the satan— who could in fact seem to be everywhere and nowhere at once. The messengers could not keep up with him; they seemed, like the news, to be always repeating themselves, and like the newsmen, only they had escaped to tell. Our newsmen can tell us a name—they say. And they say it is a different one today than yesterday. We too have escaped to tell of the last century, but our messengers seem to me to all have the same voice. Job would recognize it. I cannot quite identify it. But I wonder if there is not something shameful in escaping to tell. What does it mean to think we have escaped? That we have no part in the problem?

JOB 38-41

The Theophany: The Speech of God

THE STORM THREATENING in Elihu's speech (36:27–
37:21)—and earlier—comes upon them and breaks, and
Yahweh, who in that name and in person has been absent
from the poem since chapter two, speaks directly to Job.
God is no longer in His distant heaven, His speech is no
longer directed to His visiting sons, but He comes Himself
to Job, for He has heard the voice of His afflicted son of
earth. He addresses Job, not Job and his friends, not Elihu,
nor yet Eliphaz and the two others. God, from whom Job
all but despaired of hearing, from whom he feared yet
wanted to hear, speaks to him, and in his own tongue he
hears Him. But what kind of comfort is this?

I am not yet ready to talk about the speech of God, but
let us think about the problem the poet must have had, for
in the course of this great poem he has painted himself into
a corner from which, it seems to me, only God Himself
could set him free.[1] Job has answered all his human inter-

---

[1] Robert Alter, in his wonderful chapter on *Job* in *The Art of Biblical
Poetry*, comments that without debating the "fairly general agreement
among scholars" concerning the later additions of chapters 28 and 32–37,
"the later poet and . . . editor . . . justified the inclusion of the additional
material at least in part as anticipations of the concluding poem" (108).

locutors until Elihu with an honesty that is stark and terrible; he is made of dirt and lives on an ash-heap, but he speaks with the poetry of Shakespeare's most noble characters and the passion of a lover who will not be denied: "Yet I know that in my flesh I shall see God."

While neither Job nor God ever answers to Elihu, we may even make something of that—as we must if this book is inspired of God. Even if a large part of the last man's speech seems to be in agreement with the facts that God Himself will shortly imply, has Elihu the right to speak them to Job? Elihu is the youngest of these men, and though he speaks (especially at the end) truly and inspiringly of God, is it for the young—to speak honestly, the untried and untested *boy*—to speak to the warrior of *grandeur,* of the grandeur of *God?* Of His approaching army, Elihu has obviously heard the music, he has heard it as more than the whisper of Eliphaz (4:12), but he has not yet himself marched into danger, or embraced desolation— "Blessed be the name of the Lord" (1:20), or accepted complete abjection—"And shall we not accept evil?" (2:10).

Yet Elihu has spoken to Job as from a position superior to Job, and this must leave the reader of the poem—even if he agrees with Elihu's thinking—not liking him much. And this is so not only because we have God's word on the superiority of Job to every man on earth, but because the reader might very well know what it is like to be inspired by the heavenly music, to have heard it clearly and want to run to the battle, and even be able to speak of it boldly and beautifully—and then to have failed and fallen, and to hear the music still, but softer and going away, and to know in disgust that he cannot catch up with the drummer, that he has failed—and lives to tell about it. The boy's speech, under

the conditions of real life—especially the real life of Job—
sounds presumptuous. We are tempted to think of Elihu
what Eliphaz said of Job: "Your words encourage many,
but, look, it befalls you and you falter" (4:4–5). We wait for
it to befall him. I think that my own dislike for Elihu arises
from this. I know that Job on his ash-heap has a firm grasp
of something I lost hold of long ago; but I must admire
him for having it so long into life under conditions propi-
tious for abandoning it. Elihu, on the other hand—I am
almost tempted to set about testing him—except I know
who is speaking there too; I remember some phrases from
chapters one and two—"but reach out and touch . . . and
then you will see. . . ."

It cannot be the purpose of any great poet to lead a
reader so close to sin and then leave him, but particularly
not in a poem inspired by God. This is a problem an
inspired poet would feel, for when the ultimate truth is
spoken in a poem it must be spoken in such a way, and in
such a setting, that even the weakest in the audience must
have no passional hesitation or quibble in affirming it,
accepting it wholly, loving it without reservation—the
bruised reed is not broken, nor the smoldering wick
quenched (Is 42:3). The purpose of poetry is to teach all
the stars how to sing, and presuming they remember, to
bring all mankind into the chorus: *Diesen Küß der ganzen
Welt!*[2] And so, given Job's position, given what has been visited upon him like whom there is no other upon the earth,
who on earth could have rightly answered him? What character could the poet have invented of suitable age and wis-

---

[2] Thus, at any rate, says Schiller, in the "Ode to Joy."

dom—more wise, more steeped in good age than him like whom there is no one upon earth?

This was the poet's problem—the long speeches have only made it worse and more obvious, and before it I stand aghast, for in order to solve the poet's problem God Himself must come to answer. The problem was present from the beginning; for once Job is described as he whom no one is like upon earth, it is clear that any teacher or comforter must come from elsewhere. It is not Elihu. The torturous and torturing dialogue makes us feel this demand, makes us want it with Job. This book was originally written in real blood and real tears and in its ending a man's real prayer is really answered, for Yahweh Himself comes to speak with him. What other prayer is there? Or what other answer could satisfy?

And who, if God came to his house, would complain? Or who, having heard His voice next to him, would wish it to speak differently?

> I lay my hand on my mouth;
> I have spoken once, I will not reply;
> Twice, but I will say no more. (40:4-5)

For what is a man that the Almighty should deign to answer him—which He does, to Job, who has been tested and has won? And let us remember that, by winning, Job has vindicated God's faith in a creature of dust to the very face of that wayward son of heaven known as Satan. And Job will not speak; I cannot help thinking that it is for wonder at what is revealed.

Yet there are readers and critics who find God's speech disappointing or worse, who consider it that version of an *argumentum ad baculum* (argument to the fist) than which none greater can be conceived. Jung, for example, says, "God does not want to be just; he merely flaunts might over right. Job could not get that into his head, because he looked upon God as a moral being."[3] I think that Dr Jung has not suffered sufficiently, or even suffered sufficiently through the reading of this book, but has skimmed to the end and so found it unsatisfactory. This is not the fault of the poet.

Let us recall, in this regard, how Job began his suffering: "The Lord gave and the Lord has taken away; blessed be the name of the Lord" (1:21). From what depth of being did this come? Was it just the immediate and obvious— "Naked I came forth from my mother's womb, and naked I shall return"? A naked tautology? A, therefore A? Or did we hear in it something from somewhere deeper, infinitely distant—an utter nowhere: *ex nihilo*? These two phrases were Job's *first* words: for his life *and* his desolation, for the whole of it, for the entirety of this being called out of nothing which is his. Many modern philosophers think Nietzsche was onto something when he proposed as the great test of a life-affirming philosophy the eternal recurrence of the same. Job has suffered nothing so esoteric as this proposal, and he says, "blessed be the name…" Those first words are glorious because they reach back into this truth of all being: out of nothing. If we heard that resonance, if that resonance was present to amaze us in *Job*'s first chapter, what should we wish for now except that that which was once undertone or overtone in this book's music should come forth as its open melody? And who could make that happen?

---

[3] Jung, "Job," 378.

Not merely "naked I came," not merely out of the dust of the earth, for the dust itself comes to be out of nothing: so we are. Now then: what is man that You should be mindful of him, or the son of man that You should care for him?

Could God Himself *say* His answer? Could He put it in words? Can the Answer speak an answer, and can that speech satisfy to the depth from which Job himself first spoke? Could he tell Job a "what" or a "why" that would satisfy him? Resolve, as Jung wishes, a "problem" of evil? Job wants something else than a catechism; he hungers for God Himself, and God's being there, in his suffering, is enough—but what am I saying? God's presence, Yahweh's answer to Job's call, is such an exorbitant superabundance that Job—he whom there is no one like upon the earth—collapses immediately. It is good that God does not answer the question directly, for we are used to words, and their broken capabilities are friendly to us. Words are not this Being; they are not really beings at all. We would settle down and live with them, if we could. We would pass them among ourselves like catechismal coins until they were mere counters, and then we should be even more comfortable with them—with their original face worn off. But can the soul made in the image of God be satisfied so? Or can such a being only be satisfied with the Reality?

Job could not be satisfied with words: words have become so much egg albumen to him (6:6–7). I shall not speak for myself. Job is already happy; the Lover has come: "And I shall ask questions of You and You shall answer"(42:4), but the questions Job will ask now that God is here, they are not about his suffering—no, they will be about You, O my true love, for what beloved would speak of his own suffering to the lover who has come? What could I wish for but greater knowledge and love of You? Of what in myself should I speak? It is You through whom I am. "I lay my hand on my mouth."

⊕

But even if we are not reading through all this dialogue, and so perhaps miss the poetic problem, and the terror to which Job has stood up, which builds our surety in the impossibility of any ordinary answer and prepares for the dissolution of any complaint when the lover appears—for what has Job held on to but for this?—even skipping to this part, having read the interlocutory speeches in a distant time, and coming back to pick this part up: what a roll of speech! A speech which even the most impoverished translation cannot muffle, as the feet of man cannot trod out the grandeur of God from creation—and any reasonable translation makes this inspiring to Beethoven and Schiller, as no doubt it was. I find myself boggled and thwarted at this speech, I have nothing to say but to repeat it, nothing to speak save repetition, except in hope of this line: Were you there?

> Who laid its cornerstone,
> While all the morning stars sang together,
> And all the sons of God exulted? (38:6ff)

In this sentence lies the deepest consolation—but how can it be called that?—the deepest glory available to Job. For he himself is the stone next to the corner, or actually himself a part of that cornerstone, who is figured later in the suffering servant of Isaiah, and in the Rabbinic tradition of the Lamed-Vov,[4] and then in he who comes.

---

[4] For further reading, let me suggest *The Last of the Just*, by André Schwarz-Bart.

Thus says the Lord:
Here is My servant whom I uphold,
My chosen one with whom I am pleased,
upon whom I have put My spirit;
he shall bring forth justice to the nations,
not crying out, not shouting,
not making his voice heard in the street…
I, the Lord, have called you for the victory of justice,
I have grasped you by the hand;
I formed you, and set you
as a covenant of the people,
a light for the nations. (Isaiah 42:1–3, 6–7)

Job himself is a part of that stone over which all the sons of God dance in exultation; he himself is one with such a glory: for the world was made for just this kind of being— that which Job has shown himself to be. This glory is the glory. The cornerstone in which Job himself participates is more marvelous than any coming astonishment, for here is a mortal being who not only knows of something greater than any power, faster than any material speed, but is the sign and act of its bringing forth: Justice. He acts justly under all persecution; he remains upright under every blow of the Adversary. I have nothing; I even collapse under comfort and opportunities for pleasure, but I see that this is the deep-set socket in which the doors of the universe open to all the wonders God lists in His showing to Job—and others He cannot show. Without this being—the Man-Cornerstone, the Christ whom Job prefigures and is a member of—the universe is merely a grocery list of oddities without order. But the whispered word of this sets everything in order, and fills me with hope, for though I am far distant from Job, I hear the door turning, and I can see: the capstone of the cathedral is visible even from where I am; the cornerstone is made of such dust as I am, and the music which fills this cathedral moves even the grout to praise at the gift of being here.

In the course of his speeches, God makes it clear that love without cause is the very cause and structure of creation; it is the single purpose of Providence. That love extends from the sockets of the earth through the fretted fire of heaven and encompasses Leviathan (41:1–8), Behemoth (40:15–24), and the birds; it cares for the fledgling raven (38:41) as for the buffalo (39:9–12); and even the most monstrous creature God plays with like a beloved pet, and could put on a leash for His children (41:5). Let us not quibble about whether these beasts are the crocodile and hippopotamus, or the elephant and the whale, or mythical fabulous beasts of an ancient people. For what could the mind of man imagine more fabulous than the beasts we now know once to have been carving deep roads in the oceans, or thundering on a misty savannah, larger than the house I am sitting in? They are all from His hand; His only the decisive sword (40:19).

Job, in refusing to curse God and die, had been aligned with that purpose embodied in all creation—with the love that steers the stars and made them be. This is to say that Job's faith has been exhibited in what he did and in what he did not do, though in the course of this long theological debate we, at least, very nearly lost track of the point. Perhaps he has even been driven by his interlocutors' constant accusation to the sin of presuming that his righteousness is earnest money to which God must pay attention. God's questions to Job do indicate His power, which is why some readers think that Job is merely cowed. But they also indicate God's steadfast unremitting love, a love which ranges from the smallest mite to careful design of the inner workings of Behemoth and that vast, explosive moving structure we call the universe: 93 billion light years, and expanding! Wonder should be our daily bread. That is the depth of God's power, and the extent of His love for all things. In all of time thus far it is not yet measured. Job had confessed in chapter 31 that the fact that the Lord had fashioned the servant (13), every poor man (15), widow (16), orphan (17–18) and even his enemies (29–30), even as he had knit together Job's own bones and sinews (31:15, 10:10–12), was reason and cause for his covenant with each. But that God's steadfast love extends to absolutely all that He creates, breaks him—and us—open to something far greater than justice.

This wonder is not available to the beast or the bird—though they partake in it, but only to one who can know Justice—the power exceeding all power, and setting all beneath it in order. Our love could not cover such a range as to create such things out of nothing, and know them as intimately as pets. Our love and justice is too much mixed with fear and desire. And our word—"power"—ever has inklings of comparison, and shadows thereof, which cannot even approach if we are thinking He who is. We know how the mite and the monster affect us, but do we know them in themselves, as God knows them and made them to be— very good? Can we love them into being? Would we think to do so? Why not all these? It is injustice to creation to measure it according to our imagination and hopes. Why the birds?—to flit, or soar. Why Leviathan?—to play with.

> Were you there when I laid the foundations of earth?
> Tell me, if you know so much.

Who drafted its dimensions? Surely you know.
Who stretched the line over it?
On what are its sockets sunk,
Who laid its cornerstone
While all the morning stars sang together,
And all the sons of God exulted? (38:4–7)

Where is the way to light's dwelling,
Darkness, where its abode,
That you may guide it to its bourne,
Show it the way to go home? (38:19–20)

Having built it, does He not care for it? Feeding the
raven and the lion cub, will He not feed Job that particular
food which his soul craves? Are not two sparrows sold for a
farthing? He does come, and He reminds Job of the depth
and extent of His care, and Job, like whom there is no one
upon the earth, seeing it all laid before him, recalls where
he is, what the whole created realm is: What is man that
You should be mindful of him, or the son of man that You
should care for him?

I talked of things I did not know,
wonders beyond my ken.
I had heard of You by hearsay,
but now my own eye has seen You;
Therefore I am poured out
and repent in dust and ashes. (42:2–6)

In other words: "Blessed be God, blessed be His holy
name…"

For who has known the mind of God,
Or who has been his counselor?
(Is 40:13; cf. Rom 11:34–36, 1 Cor 2:16)

The Theophany: The Speech of God

As Robert Alter suggests, the figurative language of God's speech has broken the figuring power of language, which "means the limits of the human imagination."[5] We speak of glaciers calving, but what womb gives birth to glaciers (38:29)? We imagine or even know of monstrous beasts, but who even imagines putting one on a leash for his maiden (40:30)? Having been driven into himself by suffering and by the continuous attacks of his friends, Job is brought by the storm of the theophany back into the consciousness of the presence of God—as the giver of all being—in its unfathomable depth, length, breadth, and variety, all and each in loving detail for its own sake. It is as if this speech wakes him from an enforced and drug-induced sleep, not to a remembered glory but to a present one, to the permanently present glory of God in creation, which only one being can see, hear, feel: what am I that I should be able to ponder this? All those words of dialogue have been hearsay; only Job's prophecy true: "Yet in my flesh shall I see God." The storm breaks him like a jar, and he is poured out into wonder. It is for having despaired of this, for having failed to notice and be grateful, that Job, in conclusion, repents. And I must think he rejoices in his repentance.

Even if we understand Behemoth and Leviathan as figuring the satan with whom this story began (as Aquinas and most readers have done for thousands of years), an interpretation that has seemed morally required by the descriptions of the beasts, their untamability, the latter's Protean shape-shifting from whale (41:1–2) to crocodile (41:13–17) to dragon (41:41:15–30) and back again (41:31–33), the heart

[5] Alter, *Art of Biblical Poetry*, 126.

as "hard as the nether millstone" (41:24), and the creature itself the one who is "the king over all the sons of pride" (41:34), we can understand things in the way I have presented. For these also "I made as I made you" (40:15), and though we may not tame them, the Lord who loves all that He has made can: "Whatever is, under all of heaven, is mine" (41:11); the unbreakable, illimitable love of God, even invites the satan into his presence: has He been playing with him? And Job, Job is essential to God's love for all creation: his prayer will be accepted for all those friends who have proven foolish. Their name is legion.

JOB 42

Conclusion of Job's Story

SO JOB REPENTS in dust and ashes. Perhaps in saying so he redoubles the dust and ashes he already sits upon. In any case, it is not fear that calls him to repentance, but wonder, amazement, love. And part of the wonder seems to be that God has concerned Himself with Job so far as to show Himself to him, that the maker of the universe and He who plays with Leviathan, He who can do all things (42:2), takes note of the speaking dust. I think that Job's repentance must be of forgetting to wonder, and so, under the onslaught of his comforters, having learned how not to sing—but singing is the first response of all the sons of heaven to the works of God. That praise is renewed every morning, as once, in another life it seems, Job's sacrifices were offered. Job relearns wonder. So even as he repents, God justifies Job to the comforters, saying to Eliphaz, "My anger burns against you and your two friends; for you have not spoken truth of Me, as did Job, My servant" (42:7). The story of immanent retributive justice, of God's direct payment for sin and for justice, is hereby condemned as false; the story that earthly happiness is directly connected to virtue is a lie for which an extraordinary holocaust must be offered by the suffering just man on behalf of those having spoken and judged according to it. A large part of Job's suffering has been that judgement, a judgement not only voiced by those friends

185

here gathered but echoing in the absence of all who no longer even see the man, much less greet him. And before the story continues we should ask ourselves whether or not here—God having shown Himself to Job in his flesh—here, still diseased and desolate, Job must not have some extraordinary kind of happiness. Perhaps happiness is not the right word, perhaps it must be something with a less earthly sound; is Job, here on his ash heap, not blessed?

> The Lord gave, and the Lord took away.
> Blessed be the name of the Lord. (1:21)

These opening words revealed the secret, which we can now, perhaps, see more clearly. God creates and orders all things to the good, that highest good—Himself. But creatures of reason and will can prefer things lower in the order to that which is highest, can prefer those things without which one may live rightly—children, wealth, health—to things without which no one lives rightly—justice, courage, wonder. Yes, wonder is required. The first sort may be taken away despite our willing; the second can only be lost by our own will to lose them, to prefer something else in their stead. I wonder if the greatest of all goods—God Himself—can be altogether lost even by our willing, for as long as we have life we have a good given by Him; He is present in and behind that good, and Job is unwilling to curse God and die. He holds to the highest, and holds to that One's blessedness and ordering, as well as to his own justice—which he wills not ever to abandon. He has, according to God's own word, the highest of those goods which can only be lost by willing to lose them: justice. His answer to trouble confesses where all good comes from and by whom all goods are ordered, and to what end: blessedness. This he wishes to know, and he receives it: God comes to him.

To know that one's business is always with God is to know that one's words and action are always to be dressed in the cope of praise. And one of the conditions for the possibility of praise is a freedom which has always already escaped from subjection to the purposed terrors of history or the unpurposed horrors of accident and wandering sin; a freedom which does not require the wonder of material wealth, or the abjection of a poverty with nothing to lose. This freedom comes with recognizing the real order of good, and its source. Job at the end is like Job throughout his life, conscious that all his dealings are with God; *therefore* he is blessed, whatever those dealings may be. This is what he says, he whom there is no one like upon the earth; this is what he holds to, and having thought it lost, he complained, but even his complaint speaks truly of God, for it wells up from the requirement for His presence—and Job's complaint, from this source, is answered. And that is the only answer that is possible. Ever. Who thinks otherwise cannot offer sufficient sacrifice for himself.

And after it has been revealed to be a trial, after his innocence is justified by God Himself, and his prayer for his comforters' forgiveness accepted, and his fortune increased twofold over what it was, then come all Job's brothers and sisters and former acquaintances to console and to comfort (42:9–11). And this last little touch, in this, which scholars consider the original ending of the book, makes the story seem like it might be historically true. It is so much like historical and social reality that it seems to be one with it. In trouble, no one; in wealth, all one's old friends and forgotten relatives. Even here Job exhibits his perfection and difference, for Job *welcomes* them—he truly is like no one else upon the earth; and he eats with them—for he is like no one else upon the earth; and knowing that it is God he deals with, accepts good from them as he had accepted their abandonment—for he is like no one else upon the earth. His heart has not been ruined for what we call happiness in the world because he has not really considered the struggle and the sorrow to be of the world or in the world. He cannot take the world's torment to heart—as, perhaps, Primo Levi did (and I name him here in sorrow and knowing that in comparison I am a boy)—because his heart is not set there.[1] When the world returns to him, he can accept it with joy, knowing whence all of it comes.

The probably much later ending (42:12–17), with the doubling of flocks, and the renewal of youth and children, and the fullness of days, feels like a cheat to many readers. It is hard to accept that the earlier children can be replaced and so the sorrow of loss be washed away and all is now right with the world. It is also difficult to consider that after God Himself has appeared, more can be added—except that we are human, we cannot live human life without our brothers and sisters and children. And they are irreplaceable. This late added ending does seem to cheat on those points. Perhaps this scribe is a smaller poet—he has not suffered the enlarging *Job* and *Job*'s author intends; this is his attempt to close with a clearer symbol of Job's upwelling of joy.

But perhaps we should consider Aquinas's interpretation:

---

[1] Primo Levi, like Elie Wiesel, survived Auschwitz and wrote several books and short stories concerning it; it is said, officially, that he killed himself at the age of 67.

first the author says, "the Lord gave to Job twice everything he had before," yet then he says, "And he had seven sons and three daughters" (42:10, 42:13). This signifies that "the children whom he had had had not totally perished for him but were being reserved to live with him in a future life..." while with respect to the present life the doubling exhibits an increase "not in number but rather in value," which is "more proper."[2] In fact, the only way these two sentences of Sacred Scripture can be true is under Thomas's literal exposition: everything is doubled *and* the number of children he has with him now is the same. Having come to the understanding we have only after the extremities of meditating on the whole book, and in meditating on the book meditating also on the extremities of suffering, I do not wish to trouble myself with the thought that this additional ending marks a return to the theology of immanent retribution, or—as some say—marks a singular cowardice on the part of the priestly editor who brought it back, perhaps from the ancient folk tale itself. The real author being God, Aquinas's exposition here is more suitable. A poet only has so many ways to make his points, and readers wander among them. Having come with Job so far, I wish to remain where he has arrived, and bind myself into the depth of his unshakable joy. If this "newer" ending helps the weak to see it, let it stand. Let each of us give Job our piece of money and a gold ring (42:11).

---

[2] Aquinas, *Literal Exposition*, 473.

After-Reading
On *Lectio Divina* with *Job*

A Response to Some Contemporaries

JOB, AT THE BEGINNING of his story, is already at the point which spiritual masters of many traditions might recognize as holiness. God's statement that there is none on earth like Job should be expected to mean this, if, in fact, it is God speaking, and if, in fact, He is right. But many of the best-known readers and scholars seem of the opinion that God is a rather simple character, not only one incapable of irony (much less heart-stopping beauty), but also one with less understanding of the spiritual life than a modern psychologist, literary critic, or even his own wayward child, the Adversary. There is no reason to suspect such readers of telling the truth, and there are good reasons to suspect that they are not. First and most important among those reasons is that most such readers are not opening themselves to prayer in their reading, not opening themselves to God to allow him to work, but seeking something of their own: a treatise, psychological, literary, or philosophical. They labor in vain, however well it may sell.

It might be helpful here to bring together some of our previous considerations, considerations which have arisen through this *lectio divina*, rather than from some philosophical or catechetical-theological aim, or psychological theory. Job's fatherhood, we have seen, is under the mark of perfection: three daughters and seven sons. The perfection of his love as their father has spread like ripples in a calm lake, into the lives of his children: "His sons used to take turns giving feasts, sending invitations to their three sisters to eat and drink with them. And when each feast had run its course, Job would send for them and sanctify them, rising early and offering holocausts for every one of them.... This Job did habitually" (1:4–5). His fatherhood is not merely his own doing, as he shows by calling all his children together in grateful worship of Him who made him father, gave him sons and daughters, and through whom such festivals of love as they themselves give are possible. Through whom only such festivals are possible. The sons carry on the father's love after they have left his home; they do not forget their own, but remember them regularly, inviting them all into their own homes.

This opening theme is continued as the next character—God—is introduced: "One day, when the sons of God came to present themselves..." (1:6). God, too, is a father, with many more sons—of many different sorts. Should we think God is any less loving than his servant Job? Any less a father? Any less concerned with the well-being of his children? He invites them regularly to present themselves. Now it may be, as Freud usually presents it, that some fathers just exercise their power over their weak and dependent children. And such sons grow up to teach such fathers that such power wanes: Oedipus. In a world of mechanical forces, only mechanical force accomplishes anything, proves anything. Many people think upon such practical-empiricist lines—lines of force, exhibition of power, *Realpolitik*; some of them are even fathers.

But all the sons of God are spirits, and mechanical force

is certainly not the limit of their world, even if, for some spirits—those who have bodies—mechanics is part of the real science of their work and motion. To pure spirits, however, such sciences do not apply, nor does mechanical force, whether of atomic (or atomic-bomb) proportions, have any effect at all. A purely spiritual being can only be moved by thought. We are surely not this sort of being, but many other sons of God are. And the only thought such spiritual beings can be moved by is their own, for that is what movement means here, among spirits. More philosophically, there are no movements, only acts.

So now, this satan, this son of God whose thoughts are not the same as his father's thoughts—as he shows in his thoughts about Job—how can he be moved... to move himself differently than he has thus far? Can he be moved? Perhaps the only way is to challenge him to think his thought to its uttermost conclusion. This the satan does upon the flesh of Job. His presumed conclusion is demonstrated not to be true. He has, as mathematics teachers used to demand, shown his work, and it has been found wanting. He has not got the answer he expected. But he has produced the most rigorous proof. And thought can move much faster than such demonstrations, as children bored with the demand to show their work, and everyone with wit, know. God, then, can be witty, ironic, make jokes... In such ways a student with wit sees the conclusion before doing all the work. Great teachers know this. So Socrates, for example, in the *Republic*, convinces his interlocutors that because women have human souls with the same "structure" as those of men—they have rational, spirited, and desiring faculties—they must have equal education, which means we need to have co-ed naked wrestling (since that is how the men wrestled in ancient Athens, and wrestling is for the training of spirit). He then makes a few off-hand remarks about pinning and putting holds on one another. Now some scholars think Socrates is serious about this; but I think it far more likely that he is serious about getting his interlocutors to think about equality and correlativity. He is telling a joke which makes us laugh at the literalism of the argument taken in the way it has been taken, and the joke instigates us to think about ways to get out of this particular hold.

Whether we laugh at Socrates's proposal or are offended by it, we begin to look for ways out of the thought problem. Perhaps we figure a way out of it which fits with justice (the topic of the *Republic*), or perhaps, as with most governmental bodies, we fail—and that failure carries its effects into the flesh of other partly spiritual beings. At which time we might discover something is not quite working as we hoped: the conclusion we expected has not been reached. It is perhaps not quite so painful and difficult as what the satan's false thought lays upon the flesh of Job, but it is the same sort of thing. Such indirection as Socrates practices presumes what I have said about spiritual beings—they only really move by their own thought. Of course, we can also be moved by physical forces—or the threat thereof (which is *really* only a thought), because we are also mechanical. But even when physical forces move us, as spiritual beings we are not moved; in this way Job is not moved, though he has been moved outside the wall and his body has the stench of decay: Yet I know my redeemer lives, and in my flesh I shall see God. The Lord gave and the Lord has taken away; blessed be the name of the Lord.

So then, for beings such as us, who can read *Job* and

understand that through this story God may be trying to tell us something, it is revealed that a "spiritual life"—as we speak of it in our age of screens and compartmentalization—is not an optional addition to being human, like dessert with dinner, or a sun-roof on the car. For by reading and understanding we come to see, demonstrated in the flesh, that each human being is essentially spirit, and so a spiritual life is, in fact, that whence all other activities of our being take their being and quality, as in Aristotle's philosophy a living thing is what it is and does what it does because of the soul—which may be animal, vegetable, or rational. So every human being has a spiritual life, a life of conversation with God, and from this act—its poverty, perverseness, lack of attention, or its depth and richness—all other acts of the person take their being and worth. What is it then to take up what our tradition calls God's own word with one's own prefixed intention?—an intention that extends at least to doing *something* with it, whether that something is already clearly defined or not. The tradition of *lectio divina* is a means of protecting us from this resolving of everything into ourselves and our projects. There is another, who speaks; here and always. *Lectio divina* is teaching us a way of attention, a direction of attention. A listening. This, too, is an act, though you see no movement.

In some Eastern religions, the highest achievement of the spiritual life is called self-lessness or will-lessness; about it I know little. But it sounds to me, making suitable adjustments for the radical distinction in theological understanding and philosophical anthropology between East and West, to be in agreement with what Bernard of Clairvaux called the highest stage of loving God, in which we love ourselves only because of love of God. We reach this stage through a process of dying. Of dying to ourselves. We all begin loving ourselves for our own sake and hating God for our own sake too. Then, perhaps our horizons expand and we, besides loving ourselves for our own sake, love God for our own sake as well. The satan well understands this version of love; it is as far as he imagines love can ever go. But such holy beauties as God are dangerous, and much attention or thought on them will lead us to hate ourselves for love of God. At this stage everything about one's self must die; *Job* is the last stage of that death; even the love of one's righteousness, of one's virtue, must become disgusting so that we may come to love God for his sake, and ourselves only for love of Him. Reading the book of *Job* can lead us into this, and what does suffering feel like then? I am not there yet, nor do I want to pray for it; I know the earlier stages are mixed in me: a slurry which needs a seed crystal to be dropped into it so that all that is not of that best love may be turned to crystal and precipitate. *Job* exhibits what Isaiah prophesied for all of us, should we turn to fasting properly:

> Then your light shall break forth like the dawn, and your wound shall quickly be healed; your vindication shall go before you, and the glory of the Lord shall be your rear guard. (Is 58:8)

Job begins with God's vindication (of Job), which vindication Job himself does not hear, and ends with such glory as we all are able to see. *Fiat voluntas tua*.

Amen.

Bibliography

Translations of *Job* / The Bible Examined

Revised Standard Version (RSV). New York: Thomas Nelson & Sons, 1952.

Confraternity-Douay. In New American Catholic Edition. New York: Benziger Bros., 1963.

King James (1611). New York: Thomas Nelson & Sons.

New English Bible. Oxford: Oxford University Press, 1970.

New Jerusalem Bible. New York: Doubleday, 1985.

Today's English Version. New York: Thomas Nelson & Sons, 1976.

Other Sources

Alter, Robert. *The Art of Biblical Poetry*. New York: Basic Books, 2011.

Anderson, Hugh. "The Book of Job." In *The Interpreter's One-Volume Commentary on the Bible*. Edited by Charles M. Laymon. Nashville: Abingdon Press, 1971.

Anselm. *Cur Deus Homo?* In *Proslogium; Monologium; An appendix in behalf of the fool by Gaunilon; and Cur Deus Homo*. Translated by Sidney Norton Deane. Chicago: Open Court, 1935.

———. *Monologion and Proslogion, with the Replies of Gaunilo and Anselm*. Translated by Thomas Williams. Indianapolis: Hackett, 1995.

Bibliography

Aquinas, Thomas. *The Literal Exposition on Job: A Scriptural Commentary Concerning Providence.* Translated by Anthony Damico. Atlanta: Scholars Press, 1989.

Augustine. *Confessions.* Translated by John K. Ryan. Garden City, NY: Image, 1960.

———. *De Trinitate.* Translated by Joseph F. Girzone. Washington, DC: Catholic University of America Press, 1963.

Brown, Robert McAfee. Introduction. In Elie Wiesel, *The Trial of God.* New York: Schocken, 1995.

Camus, Albert. *The Plague.* Translated by Stuart Gilbert. New York: Vintage, 1975.

———. *The Rebel: An Essay on Man in Revolt.* Translated by Anthony Bower. New York: Vintage, 1991.

Dostoevsky, Fyodor. *The Brothers Karamazov.* Translated by Constance Garnett. New York: Modern Library, 1996.

Eliot, T.S. "Ash Wednesday." In *T.S. Eliot: The Complete Poems and Plays.* New York: Harcourt, Brace and World, 1962.

Girard, René. *Job: The Victim of His People.* Translated by Yvonne Freccaro. Stanford: Stanford University Press, 1987.

Gregory the Great. *Moral Reflections on the Book of Job*, Volume 2. Translated by Brian Kerns, OCSO. Collegeville, MN: Liturgical Press, 2015.

Gutierrez, Gustavo. *On Job: God-talk and the Suffering of the Innocent.* Maryknoll, NY: Orbis, 1987.

Habel, Norman C. *The Book of Job.* Philadelphia: Westminster Press, 1985.

Jung, Carl. "Answer to Job." In *Collected Works of C. G. Jung*, Volume 11. Translated by R.F.C. Hull. Princeton, NJ: Princeton University Press, 1969.

Levinas, Emanuel. "Useless Suffering." Translated by Richard A. Cohen. In *The Provocation of Levinas*. Edited by R. Bernasconi and D. Wood. London: Routledge, 1988.

MacKenzie, SJ., R.A.F. "The Book of Job." In *The Jerome Biblical Commentary*. Edited by Raymond E. Brown. Englewood Cliffs: Prentice-Hall, 1968.

Miles, Jack. *God: A Biography*. New York: Vintage, 1995.

Pope, Marvin H. *Job*. In *The Anchor Bible*, vol. 15. New York: Doubleday, 1973.

Schwarz-Bart, André. *The Last of the Just*. Translated by Stephen Becker. Woodstock, NY: Overlook Press, 2000.

Terrien, Samuel, and Paul Scherer. In *The Interpreter's Bible*. Nashville: Abingdon, 1954.

Thomas, Dylan. "A refusal to mourn the Death, by Fire, of a Child in London." In *Collected Poems*. London: Dent, 1952.

Watson, Robert A. *The Expositor's Bible: Job*. New York: A.C. Armstrong and Son, 1905.

Wiesel, Elie. "Job." In *Peace, In Deed: Essays in Honor of Harry James Cargas*. Edited by Zev Garber and Richard Libowitz. Atlanta: Scholars Press, 1998.

———. *The Trial of God (As It Was Held on February 25, 1649, in Shamgorod): a Play*. Translated by Marion Wiesel. New York: Schocken, 1995.

About the Author

GENE FENDT is the Albertus Magnus Professor of Philosophy at the University of Nebraska, Kearney—the very middle of the very middle of the country. It is a place conducive to long reflection. While teaching there for 35 years, he has published work on all the major philosophers (counting Augustine, Anselm, and Aquinas among them) as well as Shakespeare, Pinter, Tom Stoppard, and has won awards for creative writing in poetry and playwrighting. His most recent previous book is *Camus' Plague: Myth for our World* (Notre Dame, IN: St. Augustine's Press, 2022).

* 9 7 8 1 6 2 1 3 8 9 6 5 1 *